THE Life-Size GUIDE TO INSECTS

and other land invertebrates of New Zealand

Andrew Crowe

PENGUIN BOOKS

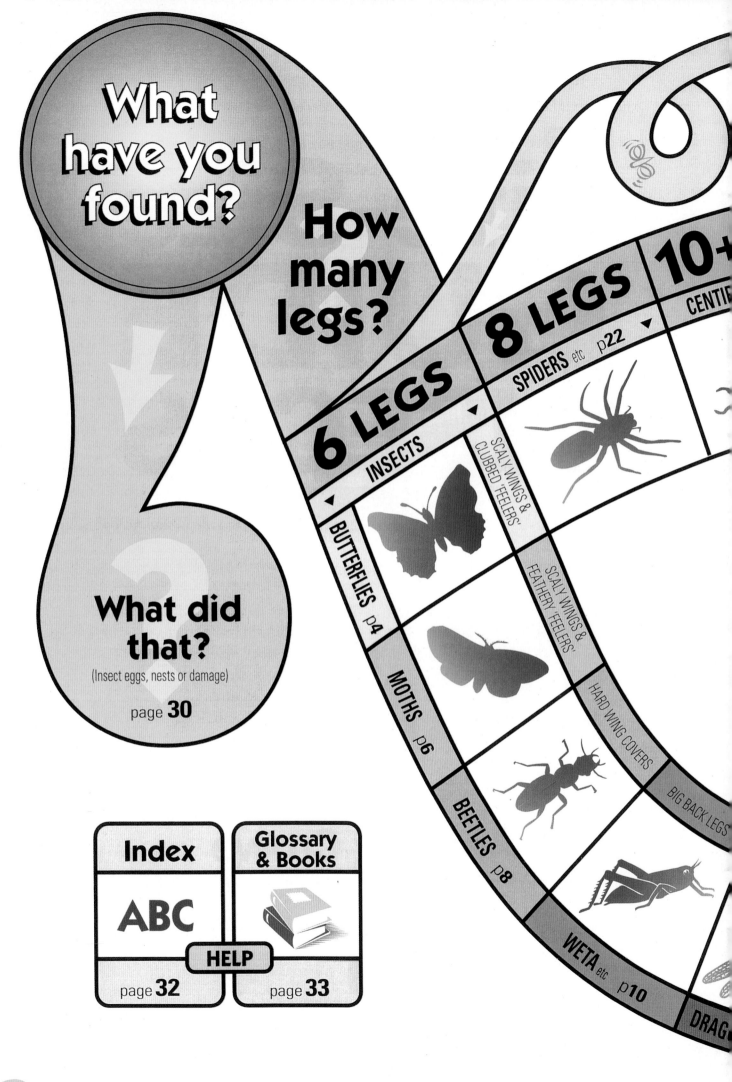

What have you found?

How many legs?

What did that?
(Insect eggs, nests or damage)

page **30**

Index
ABC
page **32**

Glossary & Books
HELP
page **33**

6 LEGS
INSECTS

BUTTERFLIES p4

MOTHS p6

BEETLES p8

WETA etc p10

DRAG

8 LEGS
SPIDERS etc p22

SCALY WINGS & CLUBBED 'FEELERS'

SCALY WINGS & FEATHERY 'FEELERS'

HARD WING COVERS

BIG BACK LEGS

10+
CENTI

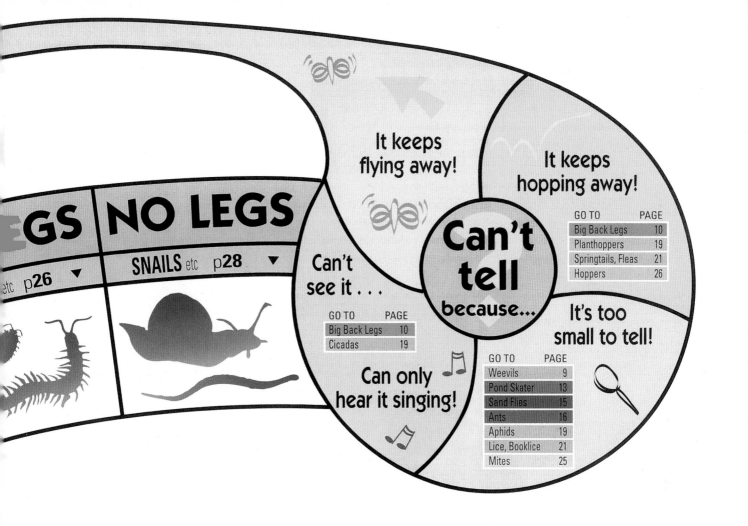

GS | NO LEGS

etc p26 ▼ | SNAILS etc p28 ▼

It keeps flying away!

It keeps hopping away!

GO TO	PAGE
Big Back Legs	10
Planthoppers	19
Springtails, Fleas	21
Hoppers	26

Can't see it . . .

GO TO	PAGE
Big Back Legs	10
Cicadas	19

Can't tell because...

It's too small to tell!

GO TO	PAGE
Weevils	9
Pond Skater	13
Sand Flies	15
Ants	16
Aphids	19
Lice, Booklice	21
Mites	25

Can only hear it singing!

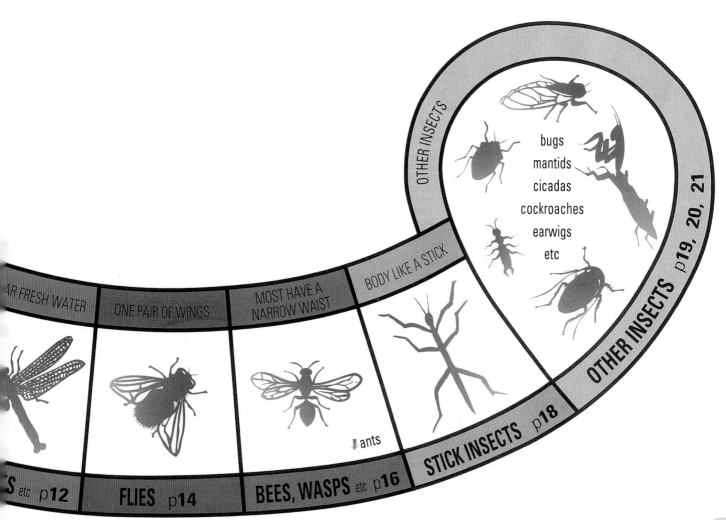

OTHER INSECTS

bugs
mantids
cicadas
cockroaches
earwigs
etc

OTHER INSECTS p19, 20, 21

AR FRESH WATER | ONE PAIR OF WINGS | MOST HAVE A NARROW WAIST | BODY LIKE A STICK

ants

S etc p12 | FLIES p14 | BEES, WASPS etc p16 | STICK INSECTS p18

Butterflies / Pepe

[Phylum: Arthropoda, Class: Insecta. Order: Lepidoptera, Superfamily: Papilionoidea]

Butterflies	Moths
• *Most* fly in the day	• *Most* fly at night
• Wings *usually* brightly coloured on top	• *Most* are dull coloured
• Wings folded upright when resting	• Wings *usually* spread flat when resting
• 'Feelers' *always* have a clubbed tip	• 'Feelers' feathery or pointed, *never* clubbed

BUTTERFLIES have large, scale-covered wings and long, curled tongues for sucking nectar from flowers. Use 'feelers' to smell and touch. Many can taste with their feet. Rarely seen in winter as most hibernate or spend that time as a caterpillar or chrysalis. Caterpillars eat leaves. New Zealand has about 20 known species (plus a few which get blown here during storms); worldwide, over 20,000. For **caterpillars**, see page 27.

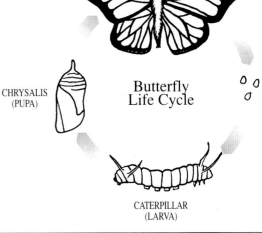

BUTTERFLY
(ADULT)

Butterfly
Life Cycle

CHRYSALIS
(PUPA)

EGG

CATERPILLAR
(LARVA)

ADMIRAL BUTTERFLIES
Front legs short, with brush-like feet, not used for walking.

[Family: Nymphalidae. Subfamily: Nymphalinae]

female

male

Australian Painted Lady Butterfly
Pepe Para Hua
Vanessa kershawi (formerly *Cynthia*)

Arrives most years from Australia in October and November and occasionally breeds here. Fast flier. Underside of wings looks like tree bark, so can be hard to see when resting. It will even line up its wings with the sun, so as not to leave a shadow. Caterpillars feed on thistles and other plants of the daisy family.

Blue Moon Butterfly
Hypolimnas bolina

Arrives here most years from Australia in April or May. Usually seen on or near the west coast. Female has red patches and more white on its wings. Even though the caterpillar's food plants (e.g. *Portulaca*) do grow in New Zealand, the butterfly is not known to breed here.

Red Admiral Butterfly
Kahu Kura
Vanessa gonerilla

Native Similar butterflies are found in other countries, but this one is found only in New Zealand. Common from middle to late summer. Sometimes survives the winter. Butterflies like *Buddleia* flowers. Caterpillars eat nettle leaves, especially the native ongaonga tree nettle.

Yellow Admiral Butterfly
Kahu Kōwhai
Vanessa itea (was *Bassaris*)

Native Collected here on Cook's voyage in 1769. Also found in Australia. Common late summer and autumn in open country and gardens; sometimes survives the winter. Butterflies like *Buddleia* flowers. Caterpillars eat common nettles.

All photos are life-size

MILKWEED BUTTERFLIES

[Family: Nymphalidae. Subfamily: Danainae]

Front legs short, with brush-like feet, not used for walking. The brightly coloured caterpillars feed mostly on different kinds of milkweed. Also known as wanderer butterflies.

Monarch Butterfly
Kahuku
Danaus plexippus

Arrived in New Zealand over 100 years ago. Common on warm sunny days in many gardens, especially near the caterpillar's food: swan plant. In mid-summer, monarchs spend about two weeks as a caterpillar, two weeks as a chrysalis and live for about two months as a butterfly. Overseas, they migrate huge distances, but not in New Zealand. One female monarch butterfly holds the record for the longest known insect migration. It flew 3432 km from Canada to Mexico.

Hints: To protect the caterpillars from wasps, soldier bugs etc, throw netting over the plant. Keep a few spare swan plants indoors. If you run out, mature caterpillars can survive on milkweed, kapok plant, or slices of pumpkin.

1. Caterpillar   2. Ready to change   3. Chrysalis   4. Butterfly hatching   5. Butterfly waiting for its wings to harden

---

RINGLET BUTTERFLIES

[Family: Nymphalidae. Subfamily: Satyrinae]

Many are found only in the mountains. Most are orange and black with eye-like spots (ringlets) on the wings.
Front legs short with brush-like feet, not used for walking. Caterpillars live on grasses and sedges.

Forest Ringlet Butterfly
Dodonidia helmsii

Native A fast flier, found along forest edges. Adult butterfly lives 3-4 weeks. Caterpillars feed at night on cutty grass and bush snowgrass. Also known as Helms' butterfly.

BLUE & COPPER BUTTERFLIES

[Family: Lycaenidae. Subfamily: Lycaeninae]

Caterpillars of some of the butterflies in this group make a sweet, sticky liquid called honeydew. Ants sometimes carry one of these caterpillars to their nest, feed it, then stroke (or 'milk') it to get the honeydew. In return, the caterpillar gets to eat some ant larvae. This behaviour hasn't yet been seen in New Zealand.

Common Copper Butterfly
Pepe Para Riki
Lycaena species

Native Common in mid-summer in warm, open places from sand dunes to tussock hillsides. Likes blackberry flowers. Fast and jerky flight, 2-3 m above the ground. Caterpillars (like little green slugs) eat pōhuehue leaves (*Muehlenbeckia* species). There are several similar species.

Common Blue Butterfly
Pepe Ao Uri
Zizina labradus

Introduced. Flies close to the ground in late summer. Often rests with its wings slightly spread. Caterpillars (like fat green slugs) eat mostly clover leaves. (Caterpillars of the **Longtailed Blue Butterfly**, *Lampides boeticus*, prefer flowers and seed pods of gorse.)

WHITE BUTTERFLIES

[Family: Pieridae]

Small to medium-sized butterflies, white, yellow or orange.

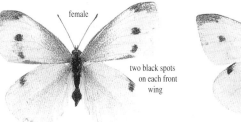

female

two black spots on each front wing

male

one black spot on each front wing

Cabbage White Butterfly
Pieris rapae

Accidentally introduced to New Zealand in about 1930. Adult butterfly sucks nectar from all sorts of flowers. Caterpillars eat leaves of cabbage, turnip, cauliflower and nasturtium. Males have one black spot on each front wing, females two.

World's Largest Butterfly

The Queen Alexandra's bird-wing (*Ornithoptera alexandrae*) from the forests of Papua New Guinea, has a wingspan of over 28 cm.

5

Moths / Pūrerehua

[Phylum: Arthropoda, Class: Insecta. Order: Lepidoptera]

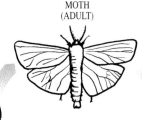

MOTH (ADULT)

Moth Life Cycle

EGG

CHRYSALIS (PUPA)

CATERPILLAR (LARVA)

Moths	Butterflies
• *Most* fly at night	• *Most* fly in the day
• *Most* are dull coloured	• Wings *usually* brightly coloured on top
• Wings *usually* spread flat when resting	• Wings folded upright when resting
• 'Feelers' feathery or pointed, *never* clubbed	• 'Feelers' *always* have a clubbed tip

MALE MOTHS have more feathery 'feelers' than female moths. They use these for smelling out the females. Like this, one male moth can find a female 11 km away! Like butterflies, most moths have long, curled tongues for sucking nectar from flowers. New Zealand has over 1,700 moth species, most of them native. Worldwide, there are over 140,000. For **caterpillars**, see page 27.

GHOST MOTHS
[Family: Hepialidae]

Named from the ghostly white look of an English moth in this family. Many of the caterpillars bore into turf or wood. All 28 of New Zealand's known species are native and only found here.

Porina Moth
Wiseana species

Native The grey caterpillars come out of the soil at night to feed on grass. In forest, they are sometimes attacked by a fungus, which turns them into a 'vegetable caterpillar' (see page 27). Adult moth never ~~eats and~~ lives for less than a week.

Pūriri Moth
Pepe Tuna
Aenetus virescens

Native New Zealand's largest moth – wingspan up to 15 cm. Usually green, but sometimes yellow, reddish-brown or white. North Island only. Eaten by moreporks and cats. Seen all year, but mostly in spring. They never eat (have no mouth!) and live only a few days. Large caterpillar bores into oak, pūriri, beech, putaputāwētā, wineberry and lacebark trees, eating inner bark and outer sapwood for up to 5 years. Māori sometimes ate the caterpillar or used it as eel bait.

EMPEROR MOTHS
[Family: Saturniidae]

Fat, hairy moths with large 'eye-spots' on their broad wings. 'Feelers' of male moths are short, wide and feathery. 6 species known in New Zealand, all introduced.

male

Gum Emperor
Opodiphthera eucalypti (formerly *Antheraea eucalypti*)

From Australia. Common north of Nelson. The moths – seen near gum trees in mid-summer – live a short life and never eat. Attracted to light. Caterpillars large with bright knobs and spines; eat leaves of gum trees (*Eucalyptus*) and Californian pepper trees (*Schinus*).

HAWK MOTHS
[Family: Sphingidae]

Front wings long and narrow; thick 'feelers'. Fast fliers. Caterpillars large and fleshy with a horn at the back. Only one species breeds in New Zealand.

Convolvulus Hawk Moth / Hīhue
Agrius convolvuli

Native Arrived here by itself in pre-European times. The Māori name means gourd-sucker – adult moth sucks nectar from gourd flowers. Caterpillars eat leaves of kūmara and convolvulus, then burrow into the ground in February to become a chrysalis. Moth hatches the following summer. Sometimes seen in the evening, hovering over flowers like a humming-bird, or attracted to light.

All photos are life-size

OWL MOTHS

Includes armyworm and cutworm moths, whose caterpillars are a nuisance in gardens and farms. Over 170 species in New Zealand, most of them native.

Greasy Cutworm Moth
Agrotis ipsilon

Native Found throughout much of the world. At night, the greasy-looking caterpillars come out of the soil and cut through stems of garden plants near ground level. Can be quite a pest. Adult moth seen most of the year flying around lights at night.

Grapevine Moth
Phalaenodes glycinae

A *day-flying* moth, found in the North Island only. Arrived from Australia in 1940. Caterpillars eat leaves and young fruit of grapevines. Appear as moths in spring. Sometimes confused with magpie moth (below), but wing patterns different.

Silver Y Moth
Chrysodeixis eriosoma

Found from India to New Zealand. The green looper caterpillars eat leaves and fruits of many garden plants, including tomato, bean and potato. Adult moth has a silver marking on each front wing like the letter 'Y'. Often seen in summer, around sunset.

Wattle Moth / Pepe Atua
Dasypodia species

From Australia. Also known as owl, moon or peacock moth from the 'eye' pattern on the wings, which shines like the tail feathers of a peacock. Caterpillars eat the leaves of wattle trees. Common in warmer areas. Adult moth common late summer. Known to early Māori who found the odd one blown in from Australia before the first wattle trees were planted here. (Two very similar species.)

TIGER MOTHS

Many are brightly coloured and fly during the day. With special drums on the sides of their bodies, they make very high-pitched clicking and grating sounds, too high for us to hear but which may confuse hunting bats. 8 species known in New Zealand, 4 not found elsewhere.

Cinnabar Moth
Tyria jacobaeae

Day-flying, common after November, seen mostly near Wellington and Nelson. Caterpillars eat leaves and flowers of ragwort, making both caterpillar and adult moth poisonous to birds. Introduced from England in 1929 to help control ragwort (but not very effective).

Magpie Moth / Mōkarakara
Nyctemera species

A common *day-flying* moth. Furry caterpillars (called 'woolly bears') eat leaves of daisy-like plants such as ragwort and cineraria. Often mistaken for a butterfly. Two very similar species, one native and one Australian. These often interbreed.

LOOPER MOTHS

Middle of caterpillar has no legs, so it makes a loop with each step as if measuring a twig. Can also hang from a branch on a thread like a spider. The moths and caterpillars are dull-coloured like the twigs, leaves or bark they are seen on. Moths press their wings very flat against the surface they rest on. Over 280 species in New Zealand, most of them native.

Mānuka Moth
Declana floccosa

Native Caterpillar called forest semilooper, because only the middle part of its body loops as it walks. It eats mānuka leaves (also on pine, native beech and wineberry). Moth seen resting on tree trunks or fence posts, but also attracted to lights at night.

Lichen Moth
Declana atronivea

Native Moth rests on tree trunks, looking like lichen. Also seen on windows at night. The long caterpillars look like bird droppings or twigs; eats five finger leaves and lichen. Found only in the North Island; a similar species (*Declana egregia*) is found in the South Island. Also known as zebra moth.

Common Forest Looper
Pseudocoremia suavis

Native Very common. Attracted to light. Caterpillars eat leaves of rātā, tawa, tōtara, macrocarpa and pine – can be a pest. When disturbed, these can lower themselves to the ground on threads of silk.

Brown Evening Moth
Gellonia dejectaria

Native Common in city and country, often drawn inside houses by lights at night. Caterpillars eat leaves of citrus and plum, as well as native tree leaves.

BAG MOTHS

Caterpillars live inside little cases (like sleeping bags), feed through a hole in the top of the bag, and use an opening in the bottom for their droppings. The female moths can't fly and stay in (or near) these bags their whole lives. Over 50 species in New Zealand, most of them native.

the bag of the common bag moth

male

Common Bag Moth
Pū A Raukatauri
Liothula species

Native Also called whare atua. Though common, adult moth rarely seen. At night, caterpillar (still inside its bag) eats leaves of mānuka, pine, broom and macrocarpa. There are now known to be two similar species.

female

Lichen Bag Moth
Cebysa leucotelus

Arrived from Australia about 1981. Often comes into houses. Female brightly coloured and often mistaken for a beetle or wasp. She hops about a bit but can't fly. The brown-and-cream male can fly. Caterpillar eats algae and lichen.

caterpillar inside its 'log cabin' bag

Little Log Cabin Bag Moth
[Undescribed species]

First noticed in New Zealand in about 1980. This odd caterpillar is very common on outside walls and fence posts but no one has ever studied it, so it has no scientific name.

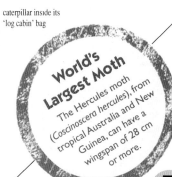

World's Largest Moth
The Hercules moth (*Coscinocera hercules*), from tropical Australia and New Guinea, can have a wingspan of 28 cm or more.

Beetles / Pāpapa

[Phylum: Arthropoda, Class: Insecta. Order: Coleoptera]

THE FRONT 'WINGS' OF BEETLES have become hard, movable covers for protecting the larger, flying, back wings. 'Feelers' used for smell and touch. Some as tiny as the full-stop at the end of this sentence; others more than 20 cm long. Many more species of beetle than any other kind (Order) of animal. More than 350,000 species worldwide; over 5,500 in New Zealand, most of them native and found only in native forest.

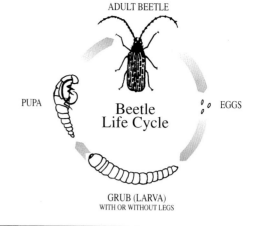

ADULT BEETLE

Beetle Life Cycle

PUPA

EGGS

GRUB (LARVA)
WITH OR WITHOUT LEGS

ROUND BEETLES (this page) were traditionally known to Māori as mumutawa

SCARAB BEETLES
[Family: Scarabaeidae]

Fat bodies, often shiny. Strong digging legs. Most eat roots, dung, or rotting remains of plants. Over 140 species in New Zealand, most of them native.

◄ Large Sand Scarab
Mumutawa
Pericoptus truncatus

Native By day, is buried deep beneath the sand dunes. At night, it leaves clear tracks in the sand with its strong digging legs, or flies about noisily (in spring). Grubs eat rotten driftwood and dead marram grass roots. Found mostly north of Nelson. The smaller sand scarab (*Pericoptus punctatus*) is also common.

Mānuka Beetle
Kēkerewai
Pyronota festiva

Native Swarms on warm days in spring and summer. Common on mānuka, eating leaves. Falls into streams and gets eaten by trout. Usually green, but can be blue, orange, red or purple. Grubs eat roots. Eaten by Tūhoe Māori.

Black Beetle
Heteronychus arator

Accidentally introduced from South Africa. Flies mostly on warm autumn evenings and sometimes attracted to lights. Beetles and grubs feed on roots of grass and other crops. Common in warmer parts of New Zealand.

Tanguru Chafer
Tanguru ▶
Stethaspis suturalis

grub

adult

Native Common in summer in native and pine forests over most of New Zealand, flying soon after dark with a buzzing sound. Grubs feed on tree roots.

Yellowspotted Chafer
Odontria xanthosticta

Native Commonly seen flying in and around native forest. Grubs eat grass roots. The name chafer comes from the German word for beetle: Käfer.

Grass Grub Beetle
Tūtaeruru
Costelytra zealandica

grass grub (larvae)

grass grub beetle (adult)

Tasmanian grass grub beetle (adult)

Native Flies in buzzing swarms at dusk in summer, eating leaves of crops and trees. U-shaped grub lives in soil and kills grass and other plants by eating roots. (The grub of the much darker **Tasmanian Grass Grub Beetle**, *Acrossidius tasmaniae*, eats grass leaves.)

LADYBIRDS / MUMUTAWA
[Family: Coccinellidae]

Little, round beetles. Many helpful in the garden, eating aphids, mealy bugs, scale insects and mites. Poisonous to birds. Most can fly. 40 species known in New Zealand, more than half of them native.

Double-Cross Ladybird
Coelophora inaequalis

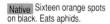

Arrived from Australia or the Pacific Islands about 1960. Has a black cross on each wing cover. Eats aphids. Also called variable ladybird.

2-Spotted Ladybird
Adalia bipunctata

Introduced. Eats aphids. Common in the south.

Steelblue Ladybird
Halmus chalybeus

From Australia. Common in warm native forest and gardens, especially on lemon trees. Eats tiny scale insects. Can also look greenish.

Orangespotted Ladybird
Coccinella leonina

Native Sixteen orange spots on black. Eats aphids.

11-Spotted Ladybird
Coccinella undecimpunctata

Brought from England in 1874 to control aphids. Common in gardens and orchards. In its lifetime, it can eat 1000 aphids.

Fungus-Eating Ladybird
Illeis galbula

adult

larva

From Australia. Eats powdery mildew, a kind of fungus common on leaves of pumpkins, courgettes, etc.

LEAF BEETLES
[Family: Chrysomelidae]

Beetles and grubs eat plants. Over 150 species in New Zealand, most of them native.

Eucalyptus Tortoise Beetle
Paropsis charybdis

Arrived from Australia about 1916. A pest of gum forests (*Eucalyptus*); beetles and grubs eat the leaves. In winter, beetle hibernates under the loose bark. Can fly.

Bronze Beetle
Eucolaspis brunnea

Native At night, beetle eats leaves of trees and shrubs, leaving 'shot-holes'. Also damages fruit. When disturbed, leaps off with a snap. Can also fly. Common northern North Island late spring and early summer. Grubs live in the soil.

DIVING BEETLES
[Family: Dytiscidae]

Smooth, boat-shaped beetles with large hind legs and paddle-like feet, hunting in still or flowing water. 16 species known in New Zealand, all native.

Cosmopolitan Diving Beetle
Rhantus pulverosus

Native Found in ponds, water troughs and edges of lakes. Traps air under its wing covers to breathe underwater. Adults and larvae eat small insects, including mosquito larvae. Flies on summer nights, making a humming sound. See also page 13.

World's Heaviest Insect

The African goliath beetle (*Goliathus* species) can weigh 100 grams – and it can still fly!

LIKE BEETLES, BUT NOT BEETLES

Cockroaches
See page 20.

Earwigs
See page 20.

Shield Bugs
See page 19.

All photos are life-size

LONGHORN BEETLES
[Family: Cerambycidae]

Flat and narrow, with very long 'feelers'. Bodies usually covered in fine fuzz. Many make sounds. Most are good fliers. Feed on flowers, leaves or bark. Grubs bore into wood or live trees. Over180 species in New Zealand, most of them native.

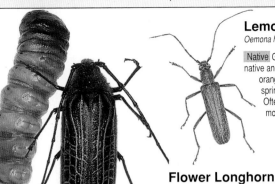

Huhu Beetle
Tunga Rere
Prionoplus reticularis

Native New Zealand's largest and heaviest beetle. Found in native and exotic forest; often flies into lights. Grubs tunnel into old damp logs, eating rotten wood. But adult beetle (tunga rere) never eats and lives for about two weeks only. But it can still nip a finger. Can squeak. To Māori, only the grub is known as huhu; it is sometimes eaten, raw or fried, or used as fishing bait.

Lemon Tree Borer
Oemona hirta

Native Grubs bore into live branches of many native and introduced trees, including lemons, oranges and grapefruit. Beetle appears in spring. Flies at night. Eats pollen. Often squeaks if picked up. Found mostly north of Nelson.

Flower Longhorn
Zorion species

Native Small, brightly-coloured beetles, feeding in native flowers. Grubs live under bark or in dead branches. Can fly.

Striped Longhorn
Navomorpha lineata

Native Grubs tunnel into live twigs. Adult beetles appear late spring and summer. Active during the day. Can fly. Eats pollen. Found in the North Island and northern South Island.

Burnt Pine Longhorn
Arhopalus ferus

Accidentally brought here from Europe in the mid-1950s. Often lays its eggs in recently burnt pine trees. Flies soon after dark. Found in the North Island and northern South Island.

WEEVILS
[Superfamily: Curculionoidea]

Beetles with a long 'nose'. Many have no wings. Most are small, with elbowed 'feelers'. New Zealand famous for its huge number of weevil species – over 1,620 at last count, most of them native.

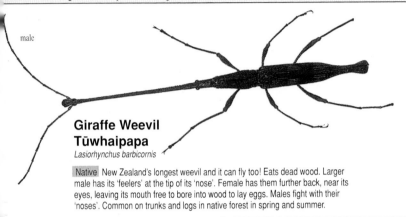

male

Giraffe Weevil
Tūwhaipapa
Lasiorhynchus barbicornis

Native New Zealand's longest weevil and it can fly too! Eats dead wood. Larger male has its 'feelers' at the tip of its 'nose'. Female has them further back, near its eyes, leaving its mouth free to bore into wood to lay eggs. Males fight with their 'noses'. Common on trunks and logs in native forest in spring and summer.

Elephant Weevil
Rhyncodes ursus

Native On summer nights, crawls slowly over trunks of native beech trees, feeding on sap. Grubs eat dead wood. Can fly.

Blackspined Weevil
Scolopterus penicillatus

Native Often knocked out of native flowering plants in summer. Eats pollen during the day. Can fly. Grubs in dead wood.

Whitefringed Weevil
Naupactus leucoloma
(formerly *Graphognathus*)

Accidentally introduced in 1945. A native of South America. Grubs eat plant roots. Adults eat leaves at night. Can't fly.

GROUND BEETLES
[Family: Carabidae]

Long legs for running. Strong jaws for hunting. Larger ones can nip a finger. Common under stones, logs and leaf litter. Many native ones have no wings. Over 445 species in New Zealand, most of them native.

Cosmopolitan Ground Beetle
Laemostenus complanatus

Introduced. A strong flier, helping it spread throughout the world. Common in old wood piles and under stones in gardens.

TIGER BEETLES
[Family: Carabidae. Subfamily: Cicindelinae]
Restless beetles. Part of the Ground Beetle family.

Common Tiger Beetle
Neocicindela tuberculata

Native Common on hot summer days, running over dry clay banks or taking quick short flights, hunting other insects. Grub ('penny doctor', hāpuku or kūī) lives in hole in the ground for many years, eating insects that walk by. Poke grass into the hole. When grub grabs it, pull it out to take a look.

ROVE BEETLES
[Family: Staphylinidae]

Long flexible bodies, short wing covers and strong jaws. Small ones (above) can look like earwigs but without the tail nippers. Beetles and grubs found on the ground, eating other insects. Over 1,020 species in New Zealand, most of them native.

Devil's Coachhorse Beetle
Creophilus oculatus

Possibly native. Common near rotting plants and dead animals. Orange spot behind each eye. Smells like rotten fish. Strong flier, attracted to lights. Named from an old belief that the beetle carried away the bodies of sinners.

STAG BEETLES
[Family: Lucanidae]

Males of some overseas ones have enormous jaws like stag antlers. Eat sap of trees at night; grub eats rotten wood. 29 species known in New Zealand, most of them native. Some flightless ones on offshore islands.

Reticulate Stag Beetle
Paralissotes reticulatus

Native Beetles and grubs found under old logs on forest floor.

DARKLING BEETLES
[Family: Tenebrionidae]

Eat rotten wood, lichens, fungi and other plants. Found under logs and stones. About 150 species known in New Zealand, most of them native.

Dented Beetle
Uloma tenebrionoides

dent

Native Common in decayed wood. Have a tarry smell. Male has a dent behind its head. Can fly.

LAX BEETLES
[Family: Oedemeridae]

Can make blisters on the skin when touched. Common near driftwood along the coast. 21 species known in New Zealand, most of them native. Also called blister beetles.

Spotted Lax Beetle
Parisopalpus nigronotatus

From Australia. Adult beetles eat nectar and pollen, often flying into lights at night. Grubs live in dead wood.

NETWINGED BEETLES
[Family: Lycidae]

Net-like wing-covers make them look like a moth. Poisonous to other insects. One species known in New Zealand.

Redwinged Lycid Beetle
Porrostoma rufipenne (formerly *Metriorhynchus*)

From Australia. Adults fly on warm days, feeding in flowers on nectar and pollen. Grubs live under bark of fallen logs. Found from Nelson north.

PINTAIL BEETLES
[Family: Mordellidae]

Common on flowers. Wedge-shaped, with humped back. 7 species known in New Zealand, 6 of them native.

Large Pintail Beetle
Mordella antarctica

Native Common in summer, feeding in flowers. Jump or fly away when disturbed. Grubs in dead wood.

CLICK BEETLES / TŪPANAPANA
[Family: Elateridae]

If one falls onto its back, it leaps into the air with the force of a car travelling at 240 km/h hitting a brick wall. Does this by popping a peg-and-socket joint under its belly. Eats leaves, pollen and nectar at night. Over 135 species in New Zealand, most of them native.

Common Click Beetle
Conoderus exsul

From Australia. Flies into houses in summer. Grub (Pasture Wireworm) common in garden soil, eating potatoes, plant roots, maggots and other grubs.

wireworm

9

Big Back Legs

[Phylum: Arthropoda, Class: Insecta. Order: Orthoptera]

THIS GROUP OF INSECTS (Orthoptera) have big back legs for jumping. Many can make sounds by rubbing their legs against their wings. They have strong jaws – good for chewing. Over 100 species in New Zealand; more than 20,000 worldwide.

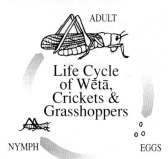

ADULT

Life Cycle of Wētā, Crickets & Grasshoppers

NYMPH

EGGS

WĒTĀ

[Family: Anostostomatidae – formerly Stenopelmatidae]

Heavy brown body. No wings. 'Feelers' often twice as long as body. Females have a long spike at the back which is harmless – used only for laying eggs. Active at night. More ancient than tuatara, wētā fossils have been found in Queensland dating back 190 million years, from when New Zealand was still joined to Australia. More than 40 species of wētā in New Zealand (not counting cave wētā) – all native. Other species are found overseas.

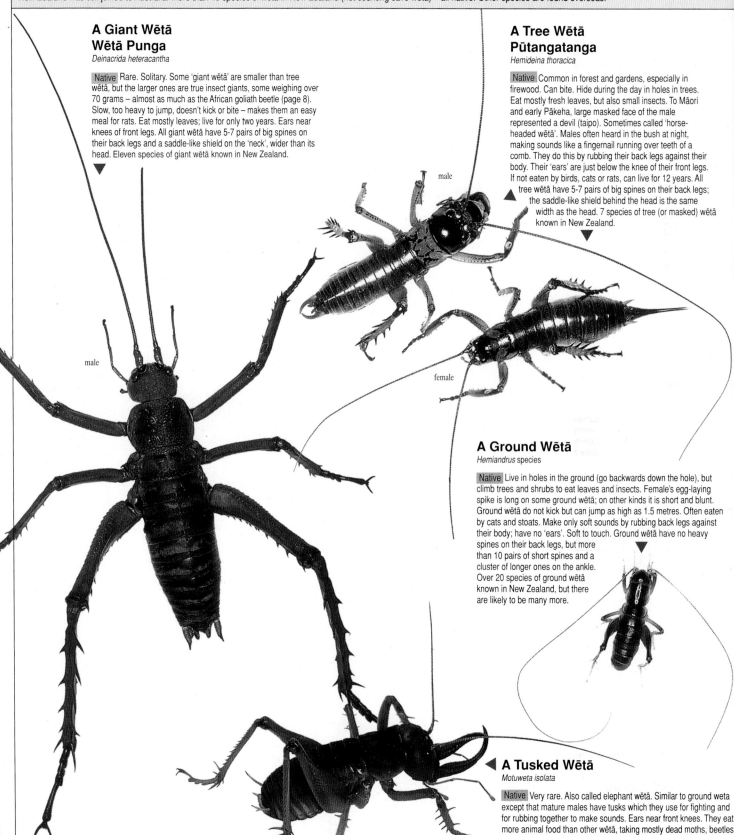

A Giant Wētā
Wētā Punga
Deinacrida heteracantha

Native Rare. Solitary. Some 'giant wētā' are smaller than tree wētā, but the larger ones are true insect giants, some weighing over 70 grams – almost as much as the African goliath beetle (page 8). Slow, too heavy to jump, doesn't kick or bite – makes them an easy meal for rats. Eat mostly leaves; live for only two years. Ears near knees of front legs. All giant wētā have 5-7 pairs of big spines on their back legs and a saddle-like shield on the 'neck', wider than its head. Eleven species of giant wētā known in New Zealand.

male

A Tree Wētā
Pūtangatanga
Hemideina thoracica

Native Common in forest and gardens, especially in firewood. Can bite. Hide during the day in holes in trees. Eat mostly fresh leaves, but also small insects. To Māori and early Pākeha, large masked face of the male represented a devil (taipo). Sometimes called 'horse-headed wētā'. Males often heard in the bush at night, making sounds like a fingernail running over teeth of a comb. They do this by rubbing their back legs against their body. Their 'ears' are just below the knee of their front legs. If not eaten by birds, cats or rats, can live for 12 years. All tree wētā have 5-7 pairs of big spines on their back legs; the saddle-like shield behind the head is the same width as the head. 7 species of tree (or masked) wētā known in New Zealand.

male

female

A Ground Wētā
Hemiandrus species

Native Live in holes in the ground (go backwards down the hole), but climb trees and shrubs to eat leaves and insects. Female's egg-laying spike is long on some ground wētā; on other kinds it is short and blunt. Ground wētā do not kick but can jump as high as 1.5 metres. Often eaten by cats and stoats. Make only soft sounds by rubbing back legs against their body; have no 'ears'. Soft to touch. Ground wētā have no heavy spines on their back legs, but more than 10 pairs of short spines and a cluster of longer ones on the ankle. Over 20 species of ground wētā known in New Zealand, but there are likely to be many more.

A Tusked Wētā
Motuweta isolata

Native Very rare. Also called elephant wētā. Similar to ground weta except that mature males have tusks which they use for fighting and for rubbing together to make sounds. Ears near front knees. They eat more animal food than other wētā, taking mostly dead moths, beetles and caterpillars. So far, 3 species of tusked wētā are known, a very small one from Northland, one from the East Cape and this one from the Mercury Islands off the Coromandel.

male

All photos are life-size

CAVE WĒTĀ / TOKORIRO

[Family: Rhaphidophoridae]

Have no wings but do jump about a lot. Most have small bodies, very long 'feelers' and long spindly legs. 'Feelers' almost touching at the base and up to 4 times as long as body. Smallest one has a body not much bigger than an ant. Found from the tops of mountains (eg the so-called Mount Cook Flea) to sea coast caves, under stones, in hollow tree trunks, in tunnels, water tanks, and under houses. Active at night. Eat mostly live and dead plants (including fungi), but also insects. Cave wētā are silent and have no 'ears'. Over 50 species known in New Zealand – all native; over 300 worldwide.

A Cave Wētā
Pachyrhamma uncata

Native This one is common in caves and old goldmine tunnels on the Coromandel Peninsula.

CRICKETS

[Family: Gryllidae]

Males make loud chirping sounds by rubbing their front two wings together. Their ears are in their front legs, near their 'knees'. Females have an extra long spike at the back for laying eggs. Crickets have been around for more than 200 million years. 5 species known in New Zealand; about 2,400 worldwide.

Black Field Cricket
Pihareinga
Teleogryllus commodus

May be native. Also found in Australia. Male makes long, loud, shrill call on autumn evenings, but stops when you get close. Hides in cracks in the ground or under stones. Active at night. Eats grass leaves, flowers and seeds. Usually jump or run, but on late summer evenings will sometimes fly; swarms have been seen 50 km offshore. Common in grassland north of Kaikoura; can come into houses. Do not bite.

Small Field Cricket
Rirerire
Bobilla species

Native. Often seen moving around during the day. 4 similar species.

MOLE CRICKETS

[Family: Gryllotalpidae]

Underground crickets with wide, shovel-like front legs used for digging. Short 'feelers'. Live 15-20 cm underground where they feed on plant roots, insects and worms. Can chirp underground. One species known in New Zealand; about 65 worldwide.

Mole Cricket / Honi
Triamescaptor aotea

Native Common in some places, but very rarely seen. Has no wings but is a very fast runner. While underground, it moves more like a little bulldozer.

shovel-like front legs

SHORT-HORNED GRASSHOPPERS

[Family: Acrididae]

Short 'feelers'. Many (especially males) make loud chirping sounds by rubbing a row of little pegs on the inside of their back legs against veins on their front wings. Their ears are on either side of the body, just above the back legs. Eats plants, especially fresh grass. Most active during the day. About 15 species in New Zealand, each with a different song; over 5,000 worldwide.

Migratory Locust
Kapakapa
Locusta migratoria

Thought to be native but also found in many other warm countries. New Zealand's largest grasshopper. When disturbed, makes a clattering flight, crash landing a few metres away. Also has a powerful jump. Few survive the winter. Overseas, a

single swarm can cover over 5,000 square kilometres with some 250,000 million insects eating over 120,000 tonnes of plants a day. Fortunately, in New Zealand it never flies in large swarms, so never causes this kind of damage. Found north of about Christchurch in rough grassland.

LONG-HORNED GRASSHOPPERS

[Family: Tettigoniidae]

Many make loud calls by rubbing tiny pegs on one front wing against back edge of other wing. Their ears are in the 'knees' of their front legs. Fossil remains have been found from the age of the dinosaurs. 4 species known in New Zealand, each with a different song; about 3,000 worldwide.

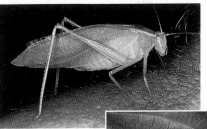

Katydid
Kiki Pounamu
Caedicia simplex

May be native. Also found in Australia. Common in gardens. On still summer evenings, it (especially the male) makes a quiet 'zip-zip' or 'scissor snip' sound. Can jump or fly. Active at night. Eats fresh leaves, flower buds and young fruit, these sometimes changing the insect's colour from the usual green. Named from the call of the American katydid: 'Katy did! Katy didn't!'

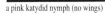

a pink katydid nymph (no wings)

New Zealand Grasshopper
Kōwhitiwhiti
Phaulacridium marginale

Native Can be grey or green. Females never have wings and only a few males can fly. Found in grassland throughout. Most of New Zealand's other native short-horned grasshoppers are found only in the mountains, most of them in South Island tussock grassland.

Field Grasshoppers
Conocephalus species

Native Also found in Australia. Have short or long wings and can also jump. Eat grass. Call with a shrill buzz. Can be green or brown. 3 species of these.

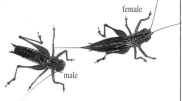

female

male

Largest Grasshopper

From the Malaysia and Thailand border comes an unidentified grasshopper that measured 25.4 cm long! It could leap 4.6 metres.

Freshwater Insects

[Phylum: Arthropoda, Class: Insecta]

World's Fastest Flying Insect
The Australian dragonfly, *Austrophlebia costalis*, can fly at 58 km/h for short bursts, making it the world's fastest flying insect.

Dragonflies	Damselflies
• Rest with their wings *spread out*	• *Fold* their wings back over their bodies
• Have a *thick* body	• Have a *thin* body
• Fly with *fast* and darting flight	• Fly *slowly* and flutter like butterflies

DRAGONFLIES

[Order: Odonata. Suborder: Anisoptera]

Among the fastest fliers in the insect world, catching live insects in flight. Some people call them 'horse-stingers' but they have no sting.
Have been around for over 250 million years. 11 species of dragonfly known in New Zealand; over 5,000 dragonflies and damselflies worldwide.
Life cycle: egg > nymph > adult dragonfly

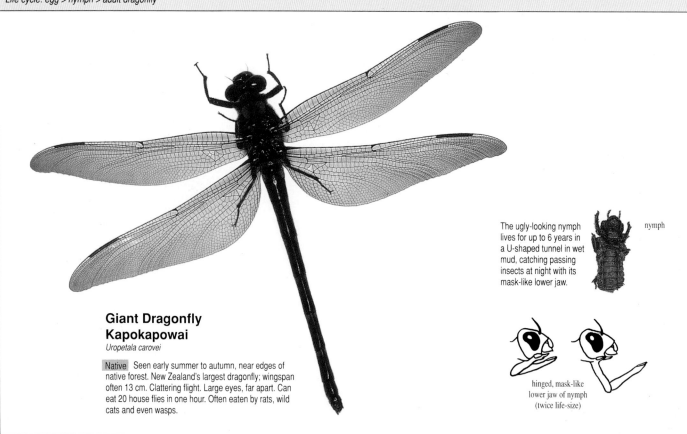

Giant Dragonfly
Kapokapowai
Uropetala carovei

Native Seen early summer to autumn, near edges of native forest. New Zealand's largest dragonfly; wingspan often 13 cm. Clattering flight. Large eyes, far apart. Can eat 20 house flies in one hour. Often eaten by rats, wild cats and even wasps.

The ugly-looking nymph lives for up to 6 years in a U-shaped tunnel in wet mud, catching passing insects at night with its mask-like lower jaw.

nymph

hinged, mask-like lower jaw of nymph (twice life-size)

DAMSELFLIES

[Order: Odonata. Suborder: Zygoptera]

Usually smaller than dragonflies. Eat other flying insects. Pairs often seen flying joined together, with the male holding the female behind the head with its 'tail' claspers. To mate, female reaches her body forward to form a wheel. Nymphs live in water, swim by wriggling and eat insects. 6 damselfly species known in New Zealand.
Life cycle: egg > nymph > adult damselfly

Blue Damselfly
Kēkēwai
Austrolestes colensonis

Native Found around still water, near rushes and reeds. New Zealand's largest damselfly. Male is brilliant blue and black; female greener. Flies October to May.

blue damselfly

Red Damselfly
Kihitara
Xanthocnemis zealandica

Native Found near plants on edges of ponds, lakes and some rivers. Male is red with black markings; female sometimes more orange-brown. Flies close to the ground, November to March.

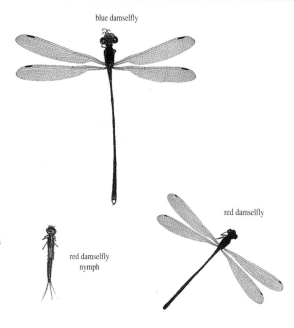

red damselfly

red damselfly nymph

All photos are life-size

DOBSONFLIES
[Order: Megaloptera]

Two pairs of large, similar wings held roof-like or nearly flat over the body when insect is resting. Back part of body very soft. Larvae live in water. Only one species in New Zealand; about 300 worldwide.

Life cycle: egg > larva ('black-creeper'; 'toe biter') > pupa > adult dobsonfly

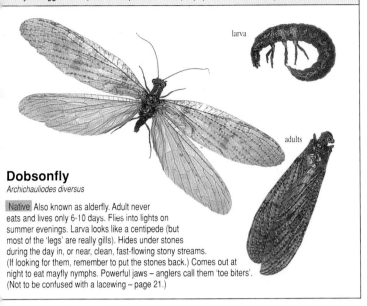

larva

adults

Dobsonfly
Archichauliodes diversus

Native Also known as alderfly. Adult never eats and lives only 6-10 days. Flies into lights on summer evenings. Larva looks like a centipede (but most of the 'legs' are really gills). Hides under stones during the day in, or near, clean, fast-flowing stony streams. (If looking for them, remember to put the stones back.) Comes out at night to eat mayfly nymphs. Powerful jaws – anglers call them 'toe biters'. (Not to be confused with a lacewing – page 21.)

STONEFLIES
[Order: Plecoptera]

Wings folded back over abdomen when at rest. Long, narrow, soft-bodied insects. Nymphs live in water. Over 50 species in New Zealand; 2,000 worldwide.

Life cycle: egg > nymph > adult stonefly

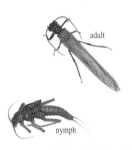

adult

Large Green Stonefly
Stenoperla species

Native Usually green but sometimes yellow. Wings fold flat over the body when at rest. Hides during the day among streamside plants. Attracted to lights at night. Short life (a few weeks). Nymphs common in very clean, cool water in stony streams so are a useful sign of pollution-free water. Eats mostly mayfly larvae.

nymph

WATER BUGS
[Order: Hemiptera]

See page 19 to learn more about Bugs.

Water Boatman
Hoehoe Tuarā
Sigara arguta

Native Common in still water. Uses its hairy back legs to row and to drag air under its body before diving. This air gets caught in tiny hairs under its body. Breathing this, it can stay underwater for 15 minutes, feeding on algae at the bottom of ponds. Swims on its front. Can fly between ponds. Males 'sing' by rubbing their legs together.

Backswimmer
Hoe Tuarā
Anisops assimilis

Native Common in still water. Swims on its back, often resting just under the surface with its legs spread out. It dives and breathes underwater in the same way as the water boatman. Eats other insects, including mosquito larvae. Can prick your finger. Some adults have wings so can fly between ponds. Males 'sing' (even underwater) by rubbing front legs over their 'beak'.

Water Measurer
Hydrometra risbeci

Native Walks over the top of water. Also seen on plants and stones. Eats other insects, like mosquito larvae. Some adults have wings; some don't.

Common Pond Skater
Microvelia macgregori

Native Common. Can walk or run over the top of still water. Eats tiny insects. Some adults have wings; some don't. Also called waterskater.

WATER BEETLES
[Order: Coleoptera]

Diving Beetle
Rhantus pulverosus

See Beetles (page 8).

larva

adult

MAYFLIES / PIRIWAI
[Order: Ephemeroptera]

Adult mayflies have no mouth and never eat. Some live a few days; others live just one hour! Delicate wings point straight up when at rest. Back wings much smaller. Have 3 tail bristles. Nymphs need clean water to survive, eat plants and are an important food of many freshwater fish. When nymph hatches, anglers call it a 'dun'; next stage is called a 'spinner' or 'drake'. Most primitive order of living, winged insects. About 30 species known in New Zealand, all of them native; about 2,000 worldwide.

Life cycle: egg > nymph > subadult ('dun') > adult mayfly ('spinner'; 'drake')

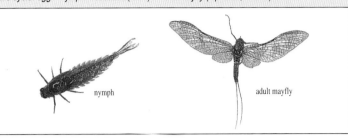

nymph

adult mayfly

CADDISFLIES
[Order: Trichoptera]

Hairy wings held roof-like over body when resting. Long 'feelers'. Caterpillar-like larvae live in water; some species make tubes or snail-like cases for protection; some species spin nets; others are free-living. Most eat plants. You can tell how clean the water is by which species are found there. Moth-like adult (pūrerehua) often swarms in the evening over lakes and rivers and is attracted to light on summer nights. About 160 species known in New Zealand, all of them native; more than 7,000 worldwide.

Life cycle: egg > larva ('caddis-worms') > pupa > adult caddisfly ('sedge')

larvae with different kinds of cases

adult caddisfly

WATER FLIES
[Order: Diptera]

See page 14 to learn more about Flies.

Crane Flies
Matua Waeroa
[Family: Tipulidae]

A few kinds of crane fly live only near water. See page 15.

Mosquitoes
Waeroa
[Family: Culicidae]

See page 15.

mosquito larvae live in water

A Note on Midges

Mosquitoes sometimes get confused with smaller flies called midges. The native **Common Midge**, or **Gnat** [Family: Chironomidae] does not bite but often flies in large swarms, getting into people's eyes, mouth, nose and ears. **Biting Midges** (naonao) [Family: Ceratopogonidae] – also native – are found on some beaches.

Sand Flies
Namu
[Family: Simuliidae]

See page 15.

Flies / Ngaro

[Phylum: Arthropoda, Class: Insecta. Order: Diptera]

THE NAME 'FLY' is often used for any kind of insect that flies, but a true fly has only 2 wings – never 4. The other 2 have turned into tiny waggling 'drumsticks' (called halteres) which the fly uses to keep its balance while flying. Flies have no jaws and eat only by sucking. They taste food with their feet. Over 1,500 species known in New Zealand. There are thought to be over 150,000 worldwide, from tiny midges to an overseas robber fly up to 8 cm long.

ADULT

PUPA

Fly
Life Cycle

EGGS

LEGLESS GRUB OR MAGGOT
(LARVA)

FAT-BODIED FLIES [Suborder: Brachycera]

BLOW FLIES / NGARO IRO
[Family: Calliphoridae]

Fat, bristly, buzzing flies, attracted to sweet liquids. Vomit their last meal onto their food to help turn it to liquid, then drink this mixture through a straw-like feeding tube. Maggots feed on dead (sometimes on live) animals. Over 50 species in New Zealand.

European Blow Fly
Calliphora vicina

Introduced. Shiny blue body. Attracted into houses by the smell of cooking. Eggs laid on dead animals and meat scraps. Often survives cold weather.

New Zealand Blue Blow Fly
Rango Pango
Calliphora quadrimaculata

Native Shiny, purplish blue body. Common in native forest. Eggs laid on meat, or sometimes on woollen clothes. Also called bluebottle.

Brown Blow Fly
Rango Tuamaro
Calliphora stygia

Brought from Australia by early settlers. Covered in golden brown hairs. A nuisance to farmers since it also lays eggs on sheep.

Green Blow Fly
Lucilia sericata

Introduced from Europe about 1870. A bright shiny green, or copper coloured. Feeds on flowers but lays eggs on sheep. Common in summer on dog droppings.

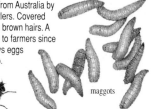
maggots

HOUSE FLIES
[Families: Muscidae & Fanniidae]

Many spread diseases by vomiting up their last meal onto human food when they land on it. Maggots eat dead animals, dung, silage or compost. Well over 60 species in New Zealand, most of them native.

Common House Fly
Musca domestica

Found worldwide. Maggots hatch, turn into pupa and then to adult fly – the whole cycle sometimes taking less than two weeks. Can fly at 6-8 km per hour.

Lesser House Fly
Fannia canicularis

Introduced. Often flies in small groups. Lands on people's faces. Common near chicken farms.

Biting Stable Fly
Stomoxys calcitrans

Introduced by early settlers. Both male and female flies **bite** people, cows and dogs to suck their blood. Common near dairy farms.

False Stable Fly
Muscina stabulans

Worldwide. Looks like the stable fly but doesn't bite.

BRISTLE FLIES
[Family: Tachinidae]

Dull-coloured, fat, bristly flies. Maggots live on live caterpillars, beetles and bugs, so help control insect pests (where pesticides are not used). Over 100 species in New Zealand.

Ginger Bristle Fly
Protohystricia species

Native Seen in late spring, flying over grassland in search of porina moth caterpillars. Drops live maggots which bore into the caterpillars, developing inside and killing them.

Australian Leafroller Tachinid
Trigonospila brevifacies

Introduced to help control leafroller caterpillars. Common. Female looks for a leafroller caterpillar to attach its eggs to. When the egg hatches, the maggot eats the caterpillar.

BOT FLIES
[Family: Oestridae]

The maggots live under the skin, in the nose, mouth and ears of large animals. Only 2 species known in New Zealand.

Sheep Nasal Bot Fly
Oestrus ovis

Introduced. The female flies past a sheep or goat, firing a maggot into its nose. When mature, the maggot is sneezed onto the ground to develop into a fly. Maggots bother the sheep, but rarely kill them.

FLESH FLIES
[Family: Sarcophagidae]

Large, grey and black, bristly flies common around rubbish dumps. Many can drop live maggots onto compost, manure or dead animals. About 3 species in New Zealand.

European Flesh Fly
Jantia crassipalpis

Introduced. Common. Drops big maggots.

SEAWEED FLIES
[Family: Coelopidae]

Breed in decaying seaweed on the beach. 7 species known in New Zealand, all native.

Hairy Kelp Fly
Chaetocoelopa littoralis

Native With their long, hairy legs, they can walk on water. Swarms are sometimes found around seaweed. Maggots eat rotting seaweed.

VINEGAR FLIES
[Family: Drosophilidae]

Not to be confused with **Fruit Flies** which attack *fresh* fruit and are so far not found in New Zealand. Several species in New Zealand.

Vinegar Fly
Drosophila species

Common. Tiny maggots found in rotting fruit and other sweet things, eating fungal yeasts. Helps spread the yeasts used for making wine. From breeding experiments, this tiny fly has taught us most of what we know about genetics.

All photos are life-size

HOVER FLIES [Family: Syrphidae]

Very fast fliers with big eyes. In warm sunny weather, they hover over flowers and settle on leaves. Many look like bees or wasps (page 16). Larger ones buzz. Important pollinators of plants. Over 40 species known in New Zealand.

Drone Fly
Eristalis tenax

From Europe. Looks, walks, flies and buzzes just like a bee, visiting flowers for nectar and pollen. But a drone fly has only 2 wings (not 4), much larger eyes, no pollen bags on its legs and no sting. Maggots eat dung and mud at the bottom of stagnant, polluted water, their telescopic breathing tubes giving them the name 'rat-tailed maggots'.

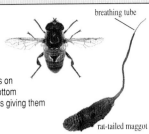
breathing tube

rat-tailed maggot

Threelined Hover Fly
Ngaro Tara
Helophilus seelandicus

Native Like drone fly maggots, the maggot of this hover fly is also 'rat-tailed' (with a long breathing tube) and lives in water containing rotting plants or animals.

Metallic Blue Hover Fly
Ngaro Tamumu
Helophilus hochstetteri

Native

GAD FLIES [Family: Tabanidae]

Fat flies with big heads. Many of the females suck blood; males feed mainly on nectar. Also called clegs or horse flies. 16 species known in New Zealand.

Bush Gad Fly
Scaptia adrel

Native Common on tree trunks in native forest.

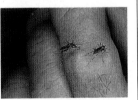

SOLDIER FLIES [Family: Stratiomyidae]

Often seen resting on leaves with wings closed, but also on windows. Males sometimes seen dancing in the air. Over 30 species in New Zealand, most of them native. Some look like mason wasps (page 17).

Australian Soldier Fly
Inopus rubriceps

A native of Australia. A pest here since the 1940s. Maggots suck sap from grass roots. The flies do not eat and live only a few days. Seen in summer and autumn, on windows in northern New Zealand.

Garden Soldier Fly
Exaireta spinigera

Introduced from Australia about 1900. Flies feed in flowers, on nectar and pollen. Maggots live in compost heaps. Seen all year, often on windows.

American Soldier Fly
Hermetia illucens

Found over much of the world, arriving in New Zealand about 1956. Maggots live in compost heaps. Seen in summer.

ROBBER FLIES [Family: Asilidae]

Bristly legs, widely spaced eyes, large claws to catch other insects in flight and suck out their insides. Maggots live in soil or rotten wood and eat most things. About 20 species known in New Zealand.

Common Robber Fly
Neoitamus melanopogon

Native Adult fly can catch insects as large as a cicada or bumble bee. Common in sunny forest clearings.

THIN-BODIED FLIES [Suborder: Nematocera]

FUNGUS GNATS [Family: Keroplatidae]

Fragile, slender flies found in damp shady places. Larvae spin small webs to trap fungus spores and small insects. Over 40 species in New Zealand.

New Zealand Glowworm
Titiwai, Pūrātoke
Arachnocampa luminosa

Native Adult fly is called titiwai; larvae (or 'worm') is pūrātoke. Larva lives on damp banks and walls of caves, in a slimy tube-like nest. From this, it sends down up to 70 sticky fishing lines. A blue-green light in its tail attracts flying insects, which get stuck in the lines. Larva grabs the line with its mouth and pulls up its meal. Adult fly never eats, lives for 2 or 3 days and flies with a buzzing sound at night. Female fly's tail-light is used to attract a mate.

adult

Maoriblatta novaeseelandiae

the glowworm

glowworm larva and its threads

WINDOW FLIES
[Family: Anisopodidae]
Slender-bodied flies with short legs and patterned wings held on top of one another. Breed in rotting compost and manure. 4 species known in New Zealand.

Outhouse Fly
Sylvicola species

Native Attracted to outhouses and anywhere there are rotting plants or fruit. Sometimes called the dunny fly. Often mistaken for mosquitoes, but they don't bite.

MOSQUITOES / WAEROA [Family: Culicidae]

Females need to suck blood for their eggs to mature. Males do not suck blood. Both feed on plant juice and nectar. Larvae ('wrigglers') breed in *still* water (and are eaten by ducks, frogs, water beetles, backswimmers and many native fish). 15 species known in New Zealand but only 5 of these normally bite people.

Striped Mosquito
Ochlerotatus notoscriptus (was *Aedes*)

Probably introduced from Australia. White bands on legs. This silent mosquito is the one most often *seen* in the North Island as it **bites** during the day; also called tiger mosquito. Each one can bite 15 times a day. Whining buzz heard at night is made by the **Vigilant Mosquito** (*Culex pervigilans*).

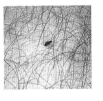

BLACK FLIES [Family: Simuliidae]

Tiny, blackish, hump-backed, biting insects. Females need to suck blood for their eggs to mature. Eggs, larvae and pupae are attached to rocks or plants in clean *running* water. About 13 species in New Zealand, but only 2 that usually bite people.

Sand Fly / Namu
Austrosimulium species

Native Found throughout New Zealand. Only females **bite** and appear to prefer penguins to people. Fiordland forestry workers kill 70 with one clap of the hands. Only bite during the day, in warm, humid weather. Also feed on nectar. Two people-biting species: **New Zealand Black Fly** and **West Coast Black Fly**, but most people just call them sand flies.

CRANE FLIES / MATUA WAEROA [Family: Tipulidae]

Long, thin bodies, very long fragile legs and long wings. Slow-flying. Like giant mosquitoes, but do not bite. Eat nectar. Common in native forest, and other damp shady places. Maggots (called 'leatherjackets' because of their tough coat) live in rotting plants, wet soil or near water. About 600 species known in New Zealand, in many sizes and colours, like green and orange. Also called daddy longlegs – see also harvestmen (page 25) and the daddy longlegs spider (page 22).

A Common Crane Fly
Leptotarsus species

Native Common in gardens and often seen hanging on walls indoors, with wings spread. (See also page 13.)

waggling 'drumsticks' (halteres) used by all flies to keep balance

World's Deadliest Fly
The *Anopheles* mosquito (not found in New Zealand) kills more people than any other insect. In tropical countries it carries diseases like malaria, which kills over 1,200,000 people every year.

Bees, Wasps & Ants

[Phylum: Arthropoda, Class: Insecta. Order: Hymenoptera]

MOST OF THIS GROUP OF INSECTS (Hymenoptera) have four clear wings and a narrow waist. Some are pests, but many more are useful as flower pollinators, for making honey and for pest control. Some can sting. Most live solitary lives, but many live in fascinating social groups. Over 1,000 species in New Zealand; over 150,000 worldwide.

ADULT

PUPA

Life Cycle of Bee, Wasp, Ant

EGGS

MAGGOT-LIKE GRUB
WITHOUT LEGS (LARVA)

SOCIAL BEES
[Family: Apidae]

All introduced to New Zealand. All have a long tongue which helps them pollinate flowers which *native* bees can't reach into. This is why they were brought here. They collect pollen into small baskets on their legs, and collect nectar to feed their larvae. 5 species in New Zealand. See also Drone Fly (page 15) which looks like a bee, but is really a fly.

Honey Bee
Pī Honi
Apis mellifera

Brought here from Australia in 1839. They gather nectar to make honey and carry pollen in 'baskets' on their hind legs. On a good day, one bee will visit about 1,000 flowers, producing just two teaspoonfuls of honey. Each hive (nest) has around 60,000 worker bees, several hundred male bees (drones), and only one female (queen). The queen can lay 3,000 eggs a day. Bees 'talk' by using a special dance to let each other know exactly which way to go to find the best flowers and how far. Apart from bees kept by beekeepers for honey, many more now live in the wild. New Zealand's most dangerous insect.

Bee Stings: A worker bee will sting to defend its hive (or if it gets cornered), but only once. The smell of the sting attracts other bees. When angry, a bee makes a high-pitched whine. If stung, scrape the barbed sting out without squeezing the poison sac on the end. Apply ice or vinegar.

inside a beehive – the beekeeper's finger is pointing to the queen bee

beekeeper (not life-size!)

Bumble Bee
Pī Rorohū
Bombus species

Fat, furry bees. Brought here from England around 1900 to help pollinate red clover flowers. Not aggressive, but the workers and queen can give a painful **sting** to defend themselves. Buzz loudly as they fly. The queen (pictured) is larger and hibernates on her own during winter. In spring, she makes a nest underground or in a tree and starts a new colony, feeding her young with pollen and honey. Her nest is much smaller than a honey bee hive, usually with only 200-300 bees. Bumble bees love the colour blue. 4 species in New Zealand.

SOLITARY BEES
[Family: Colletidae]

Seen in summer. Smaller than a honey bee, hairy and mostly black. Don't live in groups – just look after themselves. Females make narrow, branching tunnels in the ground, especially in roadside banks. Tunnels run 20-50 cm underground to individual cells, where female lays her eggs. She leaves pollen and nectar for her hatching larvae. Make no honey, but are important pollinators of native plants. Not aggressive and only give a little sting. Males live for only a few weeks. About 40 species of solitary bees in New Zealand, most of them native.

A Native Bee
Leioproctus species

Native Also called a hairy colletid bee. Can only give a little sting.

ANTS / PŌPOKORUA
[Family: Formicidae]

Have a 'double waist' and elbowed 'feelers' (unlike termites). Live in groups of about 100 to over one million. Workers have no wings, but in late summer winged males and young queens (females) fly in swarms. Many like sweet food, but some kinds prefer oily or fatty food. They follow smell trails. Some keep aphids just as farmers keep cows, 'milking' them for a sweet sticky juice. Others have learnt to grow edible fungus. 1,000,000 ants for every human on earth. Big ants can bite. Worldwide, about 20,000 species; about 40 known in New Zealand. Of these, only 5 or 6 introduced ones normally come into houses.

Whitefooted House Ant
Technomyrmex albipes

Introduced. Now found worldwide. Common in houses. Likes sweet food.

5x

All photos are life-size

SOCIAL WASPS / WĀPI

[Family: Vespidae. Subfamilies: Vespinae & Polistinae]

Live in groups, building a nest out of 'wasp-paper' made from chewed-up plant fibre. Without them, you might not be reading this book – the Chinese inventor of paper, Tsa'ai Lun, is believed to have learnt paper-making from the wasp. Females and workers can give a painful sting – several times if need be. If stung, apply ice. Four species in New Zealand – all introduced.

Common Wasp
Vespula vulgaris

Accidentally introduced to New Zealand in the early 1920s but didn't establish here until the late 1970s. **Can sting.** Looks very similar to the German wasp, but usually *without separate black spots* on the back. Eats other insects in spring; fruit and jam etc in summer. Competes with native birds for nectar, fruit and honeydew. Nest usually underground. Colony usually dies out in winter.

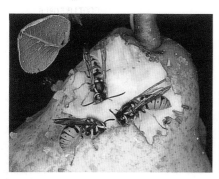

German Wasp
Pī Waikato
Vespula germanica

Accidentally introduced to New Zealand in 1944. **Can sting,** often many times. Eats other insects and meat in spring, but in late summer eats sweet foods like jam. Competes with native birds for nectar, fruit and honeydew. Nest usually underground. Some colonies survive the winter. Māori named it after the striped Waikato sporting colours.

Australian Paper Wasp
Pī Whero
Polistes humilis

Arrived here in the 1800s but found only in warmer parts of the North Island. Eats honeydew and insect larvae. **Can give a painful sting.** Nest hangs like an upside-down mushroom from branches and house roofs (see page 30). Also called Tasmanian paper wasp. Whero means red, the colour of this wasp.

Chinese Paper Wasp
Polistes chinensis

Accidentally introduced to New Zealand around 1979 but found only in the north. **Can give a painful sting.** Eats insects and fruit. Nest shaped like an upside-down mushroom – usually nearer the ground than the Australian paper wasp nest (see page 30). Also called Asian paper wasp.

SOLITARY WASPS

[Families: Pompilidae, Eumenidae, Sphecidae & ichneumonidae]

Live on their own. Includes hunting wasps (which collect spiders and caterpillars to feed their young) and parasitic wasps (which lay their eggs in larvae of other insects). Over 100 species in New Zealand

Australian golden hunting wasp dragging a paralysed spider to its nest

Australian Golden Hunting Wasp
Cryptocheilus australis
[Family: Pompilidae]

Australian. Yellow wings. Nests in cracks in the ground. Female stings a spider and drags it backwards into the nest to feed to her young (larvae). Don't usually sting people, but **sting** is painful.

European Tube Wasp
Ancistrocerus gazella [Family: Eumenidae]

Arrived here about 1987. Common on windows, or looking for cracks and little holes to nest in. Female collects up to 20 caterpillars for each one-cell nest, as food for her larvae, then seals the cell with moulded mud. Adult wasp eats nectar and honeydew from aphids. Females can **sting**.

Mason Wasp / Ngaro Wīwī
Pison spinolae [Family: Sphecidae]

Native Loud high-pitched buzzing. Female stings an orbweb spider and flies it to her nest as food for her larvae. Nests made out of white mud – often in keyholes and folds in unused clothing. Adult wasps eat nectar. Don't often sting people, but sting can be painful.

Large Black Hunting Wasp
Priocnemis monachus [Family: Pompilidae]

Native Hunts tunnelweb and trapdoor spiders. Often nests in sunny clay banks. Don't usually sting people, but **sting** is painful.

Lemon Tree Borer Parasite
Xanthocryptus novozealandicus [Family: Ichneumonidae]

Native In March, the female looks for grubs of wood-boring beetles such as lemon tree borer. Pushes its egg-laying spike through the wood to lay its eggs inside the grub. So the wasp is useful for controlling the pest borer. Don't usually sting people. Over 80 species of Ichneumonid wasps so far known in New Zealand.

SAWFLIES

[Suborder: Symphyta]

The egg-laying spike at the back of the female of many of these looks, and works, like a saw. Adults often brightly coloured. Look like wasps, but *don't* have a narrow waist. Unlike true flies, sawflies have 4 wings (not 2). About 10 species in New Zealand.

Sirex Wood Wasp
Sirex noctilio [Family: Siricidae]

Accidentally introduced from Europe about 1900. The blue females use the saw-like spike at the back for injecting fungus spores and eggs into unhealthy pine trees. The fungus digests the wood for the larvae to eat. Males are smaller, blue and orange. Also called sirex sawfly, steel blue sawfly or horntail.

male

female is blue with a spike at the back

sawflies don't have a narrow waist

adult

larvae

Cherryslug
Caliroa cerasi [Family: Tenthredinidae]

Introduced. Slug-like larvae eat top surface of leaves of hawthorn, cherry, plum and pear trees, leaving a patchy leaf skeleton pattern in late summer. Adult sawfly seen early spring.

Killer Bees
The killer bee of South America is a kind of African honey bee, accidentally released there in 1957. Its poison is no worse than our common honey bee, but their bee is far more aggressive.

Stick Insects / Rō, Whē

[Phylum: Arthropoda, Class: Insecta. Order: Phasmatodea]

THESE HAVE LONG, stick-like bodies and often rest with their front legs stretched forward. Handle with care – their legs break off easily. Adult stick insects *cannot* change colour but do look duller with age. Males usually smaller than females. Most hatch in early spring. Females lay eggs in autumn and have usually died by winter. At night they eat leaves. Can walk at about 1 km/ hour. Attacked by wasps. In New Zealand, 16 species known (plus about 5 varieties) – all native and wingless; over 2,500 worldwide. Stick insects and praying mantids were traditionally grouped together in Māori as rō or whē.

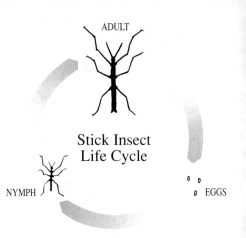

ADULT

Stick Insect
Life Cycle

NYMPH

EGGS

common stick insect on mānuka

Common Stick Insect
Clitarchus hookeri

Native Smooth body, bright green or light brown. Common – it even lives in England now! Some females can live for up to 14 months, surviving a winter. Eats mānuka, kānuka and pōhutukawa leaves. Also called smooth stick insect.

stick insects often point one or both their front legs forward like this _____

Large Spiny Stick Insect
Argosarchus spiniger

Native Long body with 2 rows of prickly spines along the sides; light brown to greenish brown. Found all over New Zealand but not common. Chews mānuka and kānuka leaves, but also needs some ramarama and white rātā leaves to remain healthy.

LIKE A STICK INSECT, BUT NOT A STICK INSECT

Giraffe Weevil
See Beetles, page 9.

World's
Longest Insect
One kind of stick insect from Borneo (*Pharnacia kirbi*) can reach across both pages of this book. Body length: 32.8 cm (or 54.6 cm including legs).

18

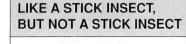

All photos are life-size

Bugs

[Phylum: Arthropoda. Class: Insecta. Order: Hemiptera]

MANY PEOPLE THINK of all insects and other creepy crawlies as bugs, but real bugs all have a straw-like mouth for piercing holes in plants or animals to suck out their juice. Other well-known bugs include some very small insects: **Psyllids** (page 31), **Scale Insects** (page 30), **Spittle Bugs** (page 31), **Whiteflies**, **Mealybugs** and **Bed Bugs** (rare in New Zealand). For bugs found near water, see page 13. Over 800 species of bugs in New Zealand; more than 80,000 worldwide.

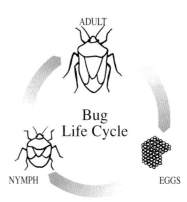

ADULT

Bug Life Cycle

NYMPH

EGGS

SHIELD BUGS
[Suborder: Heteroptera. Family: Pentatomidae]

Shield-shaped bugs which fold their wings flat over their body, making an 'X' on the back. About 10 species known in New Zealand. Also called stink bugs because they smell bad when touched.

can be brown in cooler weather

row of three white spots on back

Green Vegetable Bug
Nezara viridula

Arrived from Europe about 1944. Sucks sap of many summer vegetables. Sometimes makes short, buzzing flights in the evening. Browner in cool weather. Can also be turquoise or yellow. The young ones (nymphs) have other colour patterns.

nymph

NZ Vegetable Bug
Glaucias amyoti

Native Looks very similar to the green vegetable bug, but *doesn't* have the row of three white spots on its back. Usually green but sometimes yellow. It feeds on karamū and other native plants and is not a pest.

brown soldier bug attacking monarch caterpillar

Brown Soldier Bug
Cermatulus nasalis

Native Does not feed on the sap of plants, but sucks the juices out of caterpillars (see photo).

CICADAS / KIHIKIHI, TĀTARAKIHI
[Suborder: Auchenorrhyncha. Family: Cicadidae]

Male makes loud summer mating call, using 2 sound boxes on top of its body near the back legs. Below these (just behind the back legs) are the amplifier plates. Some clap their wings too, by banging the hard front edge against a branch. Can suck and sing at the same time, but usually stop singing when you get close. A group can put out 100 decibels. Apart from the usual 2 compound eyes, cicadas have an extra 3 simple eyes on top of the head. Adults live 1 or 2 months, sucking plant sap. Nymph lives underground for at least 3 years, sucking roots; when ready to hatch, it crawls out onto a tree trunk at dawn to break out of its old skin (see page 31). About 40 species in New Zealand, all native, each with its own special song, some found only in the mountains. Colours include green, red, orange, brown and black.

Chorus Cicada Kihikihi Wawā
Amphipsalta zealandica

Native *Green* patch on top. Appears in tall forest *after* Christmas. New Zealand's largest cicada. Long wings. Wawā means roaring, like the sound of heavy rain. Male very noisy, loudest in mid-summer, often in chorus. Call followed by 2 or 3 claps in a row: 'trrrrrrreeeeeeee — drurp-snip, snip'. Female forces her eggs into branches, leaving herring-bone scars (see page 30).

Clapping Cicada
Amphipsalta cingulata

Native *Olive* patch on top. Appears in North Island scrub and exposed forest *before* Christmas. Call 'Drrrreeeeeeeeeam n' keep a meter sweeter', often with one click of the wings included. Female forces her eggs into branches, leaving herring-bone scars (see page 30).

Little Grass Cicada Kihikihi Kai
Kikihia muta

Native Kai means 'food': they were mashed into a paste and eaten. (Māori also ate mature nymphs of other cicadas.) Call: 'zee zit zit zit'. Does not click its wings. Female lays eggs in a straight line in flax, cabbage tree leaves and grass stems. Also called variable cicada.

PLANTHOPPERS
[Suborder: Auchenorrhyncha. Superfamily: Fulgoroidea]

Hopping insects which suck the sap of plants. Over 40 species known in New Zealand.

Passionvine Hopper
Scolypopa australis [Family: Ricaniidae]

adult

nymph

Arrived from Australia about 1876. Common garden pest in summer and autumn, from Nelson north. Wingless 'fluffy bums' are nymphs of triangle-winged adult. Both leap off when disturbed and suck sap of plants, leaving a sweet honeydew, collected by bees. Although sap from the tutu shrub is harmless to hoppers and bees, honey made from this honeydew from tutu is poisonous to people.

Green Planthopper
Siphanta acuta [Family: Flatidae]

From Australia. Adults and fluffy-tailed nymphs hop away when disturbed. The odd one can be pale yellow or blue-green.

Grey Planthopper
Anzora unicolor [Family: Flatidae]

From Australia. Both adults and fluffy-tailed nymphs hop away when disturbed.

APHIDS
[Suborder: Sternorrhyncha. Family: Aphididae]

Some have wings; some don't. Suck sap of many fruit trees, vegetables and flowers. Eaten by ladybirds and praying mantids. Over 80 species known in New Zealand, including several native ones found on native plants.

Oleander Aphid
Aphis nerii

Introduced. Feeds on the sap of *Oleander* and swan plants. If you want to raise monarch butterflies on the swan plant, do not try spraying to kill the aphids, because you will also kill the monarch caterpillars.

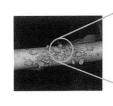

5x

World's Loudest Insect
One male cicada from the USA could be heard more than 400 metres away. Could New Zealand's chorus cicada beat that?

Other Insects

[Phylum: Arthropoda. Classes: Insecta & Collembola]

PRAYING MANTIDS / RŌ, WHĒ

[Class: Insecta. Order: Mantodea]

Hold their large, powerful front legs together as if praying, but use them to snatch flies, cicadas, crickets, wasps and moths. This takes about one-twentieth of a second! Young mantids eat smaller insects like aphids. Can turn their heads from side to side and have only one ear in the middle of their 'chest'. Wings held flat over body. About 1,800 species known worldwide; only 2 in New Zealand. Praying mantids and stick insects were traditionally seen by Māori as belonging to the same group, so are both known as rō or whē.

Life cycle: egg > nymph > adult praying mantis

New Zealand Praying Mantis
Orthodera novaezealandiae

Native Found only in New Zealand and believed to have been here before Europeans arrived so it is probably native. Can eat 25 flies a day. Usually *green* (rarely yellow). Sits on *top* of leaves. Has bright blue and purple spot on inside of front leg. Females *can* fly and rarely eat males. Adults usually don't survive the winter. (Egg case shown on page 30.)

pregnant female (South African)

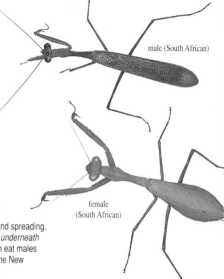

male (South African)

female (South African)

South African Praying Mantis
Miomantis caffra

Arrived from South Africa about 1978; now common in northern New Zealand and spreading. *Green to pale brown* and *larger* than New Zealand mantis. Narrow neck. Hides *underneath* leaves or in long grass. Females *can't* fly, are much larger than males and often eat males during or after mating. It often survives the winter, giving it an advantage over the New Zealand one. (Egg case shown on page 30.)

COCKROACHES / KOKOROIHE

[Class: Insecta. Order: Blattodea]

Active at night, hiding by day in dark corners. Good runners. Some have wings; some don't. Broad, flat bodies, spiky legs. Introduced ones eat food scraps and sewage, spreading diseases. Egg case looks like a well-filled purse (see page 30). Also common over 300 million years ago. About 4,000 known species worldwide, over 30 in New Zealand, most of them native. Traditionally, Māori grouped cockroaches with beetles, also calling them pāpapa, because of the similarity of their shape and habits. The more recent name of kokoroihe comes from English.

Life cycle: egg > nymph > adult cockroach

Gisborne Cockroach
Drymaplaneta semivitta

Common in timber arriving from Australia. First seen in Gisborne but now common from Auckland to Nelson. Live mainly outside, but sometimes come indoors. No wings.

American Cockroach
Periplaneta americana

From tropical America. Need heat, so common in bakeries and homes. Up to 4 cm long. Adults have wings but seldom fly. The slightly smaller **Australian Cockroach** *(Periplaneta australasiae)* is sometimes found on ships.

German Cockroach
Blattella germanica

Probably arrived in New Zealand with Captain Cook in 1769. Common. Less than 2 cm long. In spite of its name, it comes from North Africa. Now lives in heated buildings all over the world, including hotels, hospitals, restaurants and homes. Adults have wings but seldom fly.

Black Cockroach
Kēkerengū
Maoriblatta novaeseelandiae

Native No wings. Also known as 'stinkroach' because it makes a strong smell when disturbed. Found in native forest, under bark of trees. Not a pest.

A Native Bush Cockroach
Parellipsidion latipennis

Native Found in native forest under loose bark of trees. Adults have wings but seldom fly. Not a pest.

A Native Bush Cockroach
Celatoblatta species

Native No wings. Found under loose bark, but sometimes comes into houses with firewood. Not a pest.

EARWIGS / HIORE KAKATI

[Class: Insecta. Order: Dermaptera]

Flat, flexible body with tail nippers for attack and defence. Can nip your finger! Males usually have larger nippers. Introduced ones have short, leathery front wings and ear-shaped back wings; native ones have no wings. Name comes from an old belief that they often wiggled into ears, or from ear-shape of wings (ear-wing > ear-wig). Over 20 species known in New Zealand (most of them native); over 1,800 worldwide.

Life cycle: egg > nymph > adult earwig

European Earwig
Forficula auricularia

Introduced to New Zealand. Common inside apricots and peaches, eating around the stones. Also hunts other insects. Feeds at night. Hides among leaves during the day. Burrows into the ground for winter. Has tightly folded wings but rarely flies. An up-turned flowerpot stuffed with crumpled paper will attract them.

Seashore Earwig / Matā
Anisolabis littorea

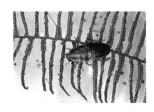

Native Wingless. Common near high tide mark on sandy beaches, under stones and driftwood, near seaweed and other plants. Eats seaweed, hoppers and slaters. Tail nippers both the same length on the female, but unequal on male.

LIKE AN EARWIG BUT NOT AN EARWIG

A Rove Beetle
See page 9.

All photos are life-size

LACEWINGS
[Class: Insecta. Order: Neuroptera]

Adults have 4 similar-sized net-veined wings, held roof-like over body when at rest. Larvae have sucking jaws. About 16 species in New Zealand; over 5,000 worldwide.
Life cycle: egg > larva > pupa > adult lacewing

Antlion Lacewing
Weeleus acutus

Native Narrow-winged adult hides among leaves by day; flies only at night. Larva (known as antlion) makes a cone-shaped pit (5 cm across) in loose or sandy dry soil, and waits in a hole at the bottom to eat insects which stumble in.

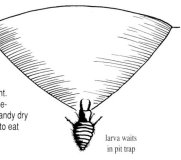

larva waits in pit trap

Tasmanian Lacewing
Micromus tasmaniae

From Australia. Larva and adult eat mostly aphids, so are useful in the garden. Found all year. Active at night. Larva looks like a flat caterpillar.

TERMITES
[Class: Insecta. Order: Isoptera]

Live in groups of up to 2 million: a king and queen, soldiers and workers. Soldiers and workers have no eyes or wings. King and queen lose theirs after mating. Queen's body swells to make a huge bag for laying eggs. Some are bad pests in tropical countries. Feed on wood, dry grass, fungi and animal dung. Also called 'white ants', but not related to ants: have straight 'feelers' and no narrow waist. New Zealand has 3 native species and about 4 introduced in timber from Australia; over 2,300 worldwide.
Life cycle: egg > nymph > adult termite

New Zealand Drywood Termite
Kalotermes brouni

Native Generally feeds only on dead, dry wood. Found from about Christchurch north.

BRISTLETAILS
[Class: Insecta. Order: Thysanura]

Flat, wingless insects with three long tail bristles. Have been around for over 300 million years. 3 species known in New Zealand; about 370 worldwide.
Life cycle: eggs hatch as little bristletails

Silverfish
Lepisma saccharina

Found worldwide; accidentally introduced by early settlers. Shaped like a small, flat fish, covered with silvery scales. Moves quickly like a tiny lizard. Active at night. Common in damp, dark areas of homes, often damaging books and wallpaper. Particularly fond of flour, and paper with glue in it.

BOOKLICE
[Class: Insecta. Order: Psocoptera]

Small, soft-bodied insects. Most are found on leaves and branches of trees and shrubs, under bark and in leaf litter. Some kinds have wings. Over 50 species in New Zealand; over 3,000 worldwide.
Life cycle: egg > nymph > adult booklouse

A Booklouse
Trogium pulsatorium

Introduced. Wingless. Tiny. Run quickly across furniture and stop, feeding on moulds growing on glue in bindings of damp old books and wallpaper. Often not noticed. Rarely do any damage. Sometimes heard at night tapping to each other by beating their abdomen on whatever they are standing on. Tapping is loudest when they are standing on paper.

5x

SPRINGTAILS
[Class: Collembola. Order: Collembola]

Tiny, wingless, soft-bodied creatures, usually 1-3 mm long, common in damp leaf litter and compost; often fall into swimming pools. Eat mostly rotting leaves. Many have a forked spring under the tail which they release to leap into the air like fleas. Have been around for about 370 million years. Have 6 legs, but are not regarded as true insects. About 400 species known in New Zealand; over 6,000 species worldwide.
Life cycle: eggs hatch as little springtails

Springtails

5x

PARASITIC LICE / KUTU
[Class: Insecta. Order: Phthiraptera]

Males usually smaller than females. Tiny, flattened, wingless insects, living on birds and mammals. Some suck blood. Each kind usually feeds on just one kind of animal. Found on all domestic animals, but not on possums or hedgehogs. Lice are also found on all birds, fur seals and sea lions. About 350 species known in New Zealand; over 3,300 worldwide.
Life cycle: egg > nymph > adult louse

Human Head Louse
Pediculus humanus capitis

Introduced before Europeans. A tiny, colourless insect that can live in people's hair. Female lays 80-100 eggs ('nits') during her one-month life. Uses a quick-setting glue to attach eggs to the hairs. Other kinds of lice live on other parts of the human body.

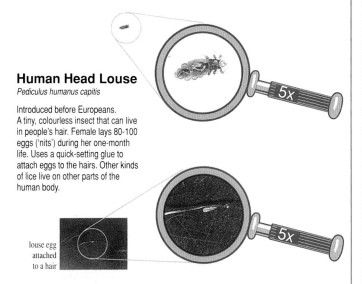

5x

louse egg attached to a hair

FLEAS / PURUHI, KEHA
[Class: Insecta. Order: Siphonaptera]

Also known to Māori as tuiau. Tiny, jumping, wingless insects. Look as if they have been flattened sideways. Males and females suck blood. In New Zealand, dogs, cats, rats, chicken and people (and many other animals) attacked, but each kind of flea prefers the blood of only one of these animals. Native fleas found on long-tailed bats, weka, kea, fernbirds and many seabirds. 35 kinds known in New Zealand; about 2,500 worldwide.
Life cycle: egg > larva (maggot) > pupa > adult flea

Cat Flea
Ctenocephalides felis

Introduced. Common in summer on cats. Prefer the blood of cats, but suck people's blood too. The world's best insect jumper for its size; one reached a height of 34 cm in one jump, with an acceleration over 20 times that of a space rocket. One flea can lay 500 tiny white eggs, which hatch into bristly, whitish, thread-like larvae. These live in carpets etc, not on the cat.

5x

World's Fastest-Running Insect
The American cockroach, *Periplaneta americana*, can reach 5.4 km/h (50 body lengths per second).

Eight Legs (And Use a Web to Catch their Prey)

[Phylum: Arthropoda. Class: Arachnida]

Spiders / Pūngāwerewere [Order: Araneida]

SPIDERS ARE NOT INSECTS for they have 8 legs, not 6. Spiders hunt mostly insects, injecting poison; many weave silken webs to tangle their prey. Most have 8 eyes. Some are great travellers, hanging out threads of web to catch the wind, reaching heights of 6,000 metres and more (where they have been collected by aircraft). Spiders have been around for about 350 million years. About 2,500 species in New Zealand (1,500 named) – most of them native; over 39,000 worldwide.

Life cycle: eggs hatch as little spiders

Spider Bites

Spiders are naturally shy, but larger ones can bite in self-defense. In New Zealand, only the Katipō (& much rarer Redback) is really poisonous, but the bites of a few others can be painful. Some people are especially sensitive to spider bites.

ORBWEB SPIDERS
[Superfamily: Araneoidea]

Females spin neat, circular, sticky webs like silver cartwheels. Like all web-builders, they are almost blind. A striking green one is often seen in mason wasp nests (**Green Orbweb Spider**) and a silver one is sometimes found hanging under its horizontal web (**Horizontal Orbweb Spider**). Over 30 species known in New Zealand.

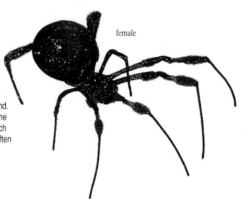
female

orbweb

Golden Orbweb Spider
Nephila edulis

Tiny young spiders in Australia put out a thread; the wind picks them up and brings them most years to New Zealand. Big. Body of female can be 24 mm; male only 6 mm. Name comes from its large (3-metre) golden-coloured web, which is strong enough to catch small birds and bats. Female often seen on her web during the day. In Papua New Guinea, these spiders are roasted and eaten.

Garden Orbweb Spider
Eriophora pustulosa

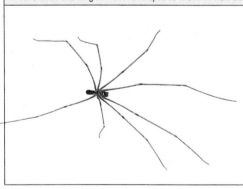

Introduced from Australia. Various sizes and colours, but all have 5 large bumps on the back. Very common in gardens, making most of the orbwebs seen there. Check these webs out at night, to find the spiders. Often rebuilds its web every night, waiting nearby holding a 'telegraph thread' to signal dinner. (See page 30 for egg sac.)

Twospined Spider
Poecilopachys australasiae

An Australian spider found in the North Island since the early 1970s. How it got here, no one knows. Female can quickly change colour; male is duller and much smaller (2.5 mm). By day, they hide under citrus leaves. Builds her web late at night and eats the silk again before dawn. Useful in the garden for catching large moths. Appear in spring.

female spider with egg sac

LINE WEB SPIDERS
[Family: Pholcidae]

Weave loose and tangled webs. One species known in New Zealand. Looks similar to a harvestman (page 25).

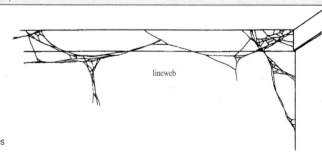
lineweb

Daddy Longlegs Spider
Pholcus phalangioides

Introduced. Common inside houses throughout the world. Doesn't usually inject poison, but catches its prey by tightly wrapping it up. If something too big lands in its web, it whirls round and round to scare the intruder off. Female often carries egg sac around with her.

LADDER WEB SPIDERS
[Family: Desidae]

Web forms a zig-zag ladder pattern, but becomes messy with age. Over 80 species known in New Zealand.

World's Largest Spider
The Goliath bird-eating spider (*Theraphosa blondi*) of Guyana, has a body length of 9 cm and a legspan of 28 cm – big enough to cover a dinner plate.

Grey House Spider
Badumna longinqua

From Australia. Webs very common on outside of houses and around windows all over New Zealand. There is often a funnel in one corner of the web leading off to the spider's hiding place. Gets eaten by whitetailed spiders (see page 24).

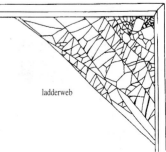
ladderweb

All photos are life-size

COBWEB SPIDERS

Web untidy. Use comb on back legs to throw silk over their victim. This group includes the poisonous black widow spider, found in many warm parts of the world. Over 20 species known in New Zealand.

NZ Cobweb Spider
Achaearanea veruculata

Native Webs common on outside of houses and on fences. From New Zealand, it has found its way to England and Australia.

White Cobweb Spider
Achaearanea tepidariorum

Recent arrival in New Zealand. Found in similar places to the native New Zealand cobweb spider.

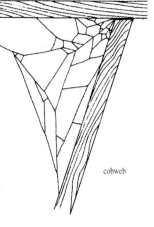

cobweb

Katipō Spider
Latrodectus katipo

Native Katipō means 'night stinger'. Adult female **has a poisonous bite**, but is shy and only 2 people have ever died from it – both of them over 100 years ago. These days an antivenom is available. Male much smaller and doesn't bite. Lives only near beaches. Eats mostly beetles. Has a red stripe on its back, but the less common native **Black Katipō** (*Latrodectus atritus*) has no stripe. Since 1980, the odd **Australian Redback Spider** (*Latrodectus hasselti*) – a more dangerous relative – has been found in Northland, Rotorua, New Plymouth and Wanaka.

False Katipō Spider
Steatoda capensis

From South Africa. Often confused with the Katipō Spider. Unlike the Katipō, it is common around houses and in the garden, under bark, stones and flowerpots. Now taking over sand dune areas where the Katipō normally lives. Bite can be painful but not dangerous.

Dewdrop Spider
Argyrodes antipodianus (often misspelt as *antipodiana*)

Introduced. Tiny. Look like specks of silver solder, or dewdrops. Groups of them feed on the back of webs of many orbweb spiders. Called 'web pirates' because they steal the other spider's food. Also called quicksilver spiders.

SHEETWEB SPIDERS

Build trampoline-like webs. In these two sheetweb spider families, over 150 species known in New Zealand, most of them native.

Sheetweb Spider
Cambridgea species

Native Body can be 25 mm long. Wandering males often get trapped when they fall into the bath and can't climb the slippery sides. Makes its web among leaves of shrubs, in native forest and around houses in the North Island, waiting under web at night. Insects fly into special 'knock-down' threads, fall and get tangled up in large 'trampoline' below. Hides by day in a short, silk-lined tunnel at edge of web.

Sombrero Spider
Stiphidion facetum

Introduced from Australia. Found around rocky overhangs and in woodsheds. Makes a sheetweb shaped like a sombrero.

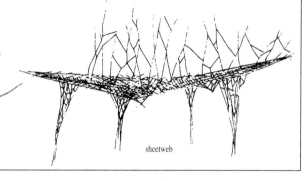

sheetweb

TUNNELWEB SPIDERS

Live in tunnel-like webs, catching insects as they pass near the mouth of the web. 25 species known in New Zealand.

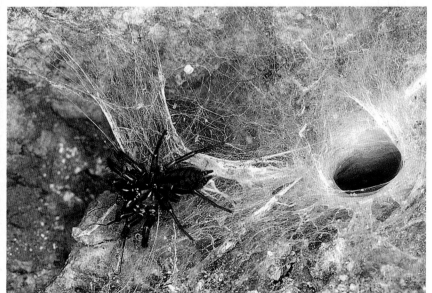

Banded Tunnelweb Spider
Hexathele species

Native At night, it waits for insects to walk past the entrance to its tunnel-like web. These web tunnels are common on rocks, under stones and logs, and in little finger-sized holes in tree trunks. To get a good look at the spider, you will need to keep very still. Any movement and it runs for cover inside the tunnel. **Bite can be painful** but is not poisonous.

tunnelweb

23

Eight Legs (But Don't Use a Web to Catch their Prey)

[Phylum: Arthropoda. Class: Arachnida]

WANDERING SPIDERS

Don't use webs to catch their prey, but wander around or run fast, hunting for food.

[Families: Heteropodidae, Zoropsidae, Pisauridae, Corinnidae, Lamponidae, Dysderidae, Lycosidae & Salticidae]

Avondale Spider

Delena cancerides [Family: Sparassidae]

This harmless Australian huntsman spider came to the Avondale district of Auckland in the early 1920s in a packet of Australian timber, and hasn't spread much since. Lives in groups of about 200, mostly under loose bark of wattle trees, but comes into houses too. Active at night. Body up to 3 cm long, legspan 20 cm (the size of a saucer). In 1989, 374 of them were sent from here to Hollywood for the film, *Arachnophobia*.

Large Brown Vagrant Spider

Uliodon species [Family: Zoropsidae]

Native Hunts on forest floor at night. By day, hides in silken sacs under logs and stones. Runs fast, stops and runs again. At least 40 species in New Zealand.

Australian Ground Spider

Supunna picta [Family: Corinnidae]

From Australia. Common in homes and gardens. With its orange legs, it runs around during the day at amazing speed, waving its front two legs in front like the 'feelers' of a hunting wasp. Moves like a clockwork toy out of control. Builds a silken sac to hide in.

Whitetailed Spider

Lampona cylindrata [Family: Lamponidae]

Arrived from Australia in the 19th century. Name comes from the white spot on the spider's tail end. In the evening, it plucks threads of another spider's web, pretending to be a captured insect. The web's owner gets a surprise when it appears for supper and is grabbed and eaten. Build silken sacs to hide in; very common in houses in late summer. Bite can be painful. The venom itself is often said to be dangerous but there is still no proof of this.

Slater Spider

Dysdera crocata [Family: Dysderidae]

Introduced. Bright reddish-brown, with an abdomen like a peanut. Legs red. Lives in compost heaps, beneath bricks and rocks. Useful in the garden because it eats mostly slaters. Active at night. Bite can be painful and slow to heal. Also called six-eyed garden spider.

Garden Wolf Spider

Anoteropsis hilaris [Family: Lycosidae]

Native Common in gardens. For 5 weeks, female carries her egg sac. Then her 100 or so young climb on her back to be carried around for another week, until old enough to look after themselves. Hunts on the ground by day, finding its way with polarised light. Called wolf spiders because of the way they run down their prey. 28 species of wolf spiders known in New Zealand.

Blackheaded Jumping Spider

Trite planiceps [Family: Salticidae]

Native Hunts during the day, by jumping. Can leap 40 cm in one jump. Over 50 species of jumping spiders named in New Zealand but there are thought to be over 100. Jumping spiders have the best vision of all spiders.

House Hopper Spider

Trite parvula & *Hypoblemum albovittatum* (previously lumped together as '*Euophrys parvula*') [Family: Salticidae]

Introduced. Another jumping spider. Very common in homes.

Water Spider

'*Dolomedes aquaticus*' [Family: Pisauridae]

Native Can walk on water, swim or dive, staying underwater for as long as half an hour. Hunts along edges of shingle river-beds and lake shores – mostly at night. Rests front two legs on water surface, waiting for vibrations of struggling insects and even small fish. Does not build a nurseryweb.

Nurseryweb Spider

Dolomedes minor [Family: Pisauridae]

Native Except during motherhood, this spider is a wanderer, hunting at night. Builds no prey-catching web. In summer, female carries her young around in an egg sac. But as her 200 young spiders grow, she puts this sac inside a nurseryweb near the top of a bush. Guards the nurseryweb at night; by day she hides nearby.

All photos are life-size

SIT & WAIT' SPIDERS
[Family: Thomisidae]

Don't use webs to catch their prey, but just sit and wait for their food to come to them, pouncing on their victims.
The spiders in this group are mostly Thomisidae or Crab Spiders, of which over 30 species are so far known in New Zealand.

Square-Ended Crab Spider
Sidymella species [Family: Thomisidae]

Native Named after its crab-like front legs. Hides by falling on its back; the square end helps it to later somersault backwards onto its front again. Often hangs on a single thread or hides on trees, waiting to catch a passing meal. Active day and night.

Flower Spider
Diaea species [Family: Thomisidae]

Native Crab-like front legs. Can run forwards or scuttle sideways. Often hides on flowers during the day, waiting to jump on passing flower-pollinating insects. Many can change colour to match their surroundings.

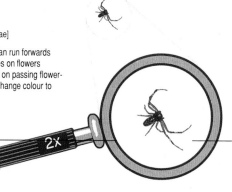

2x

Harvestmen, False Scorpions, Mites and Ticks
[Phylum: Arthropoda. Class: Arachnida. Orders: Opiliones, Pseudoscorpiones & Acarina]

LIKE SPIDERS, these creatures all have 8 legs so they too belong to the group called arachnids. The difference is that none of these creatures can make any kind of web for catching their food. They look different from spiders too for none of them have a narrow waist and they don't have poison fangs.

HARVESTMEN
[Order: Opiliones]

Often noticed in the fields of Europe at harvest-time. Unlike spiders, they have no waist, nor poison fangs, cannot spin silk and have only two eyes. Eat small insects at night and shelter in damp places. New Zealand has over 150 native species, most with short legs and hard, armour-plated bodies, living in native forest. About 5,500 species known worldwide.
Life cycle: eggs hatch as little harvestmen

European Harvestman
Phalangium opilio

Introduced. Found in summer throughout New Zealand in overgrown gardens and open country. Soft body; very long legs. Also called daddy longlegs – a name used for crane flies and daddy longlegs spiders too. In captivity, they have been fed dead insects. meat, fat, bread and fruit juice

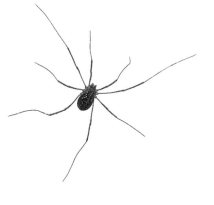

TICKS
[Order: Acarina. Suborder: Ixodida]

Biting, sucking creatures. Larvae have only 4 or 6 legs. Ticks are slightly larger than mites. Over 800 species worldwide; only 6 native species so far discovered in New Zealand – the **Bat Tick, Tuatara Tick, Kiwi Tick, Cormorant Tick, Penguin Tick** and **Common Seabird Tick.**
Life cycle: egg > larva > nymph > adult tick

New Zealand Cattle Tick
Haemaphysalis longicornis

From Asia; also found in Australia and some Pacific Islands. The adult females. nymphs and six-legged larvae all bite cattle and other large animals, including people, sucking their blood. When full of blood, they are dark red-brown.

MITES / NGAOKI
[Order: Acarina]

Biting, sucking creatures. Larvae have only 4 or 6 legs. Some are a nuisance in orchards, in gardens or on animals. They are also common in forest leaf litter. New Zealand has several thousand species (about 840 of them native), but most are tiny. Over 30,000 worldwide.
Life cycle: egg > larva > nymph > adult mite

Whirligig Mite
Anystis species

Introduced. A very common bright red mite seen crawling up walls and trunks of trees. Useful in orchards, because it eats harmful spider mites which damage the fruit and leaves.

5x

FALSE SCORPIONS
[Order: Pseudoscorpiones]

Like tiny scorpions, but with no stinging tail. Several native ones found in forest, under bark of dead trees and in leaf litter; some live on the seashore or on mountains. Pincers contain poison, but not enough to harm people. Eat mostly springtails. 70 species known in New Zealand (most of them native); about 2,000 known worldwide.
Life cycle: egg > larva > nymph > adult false scorpion

A Native Mite
Cheyzeria species

Native Common under bark and stones. A predator. This is one of New Zealand's larger mites. It is unusual for the large tufts of hairs on its body.

A False Scorpion

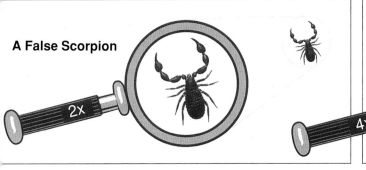

2x

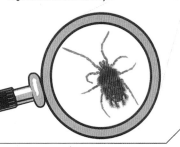

4x

World's Fastest Arachnid
When hunting lizards, wind scorpions [Order: Solifugae] from the semi-desert regions of Africa and the Middle East can reach speeds over 16 km/hr.

Ten Legs or More

[Phyla: Arthropoda & Onychophora]

Centipedes	Millipedes
• One pair of legs per body segment • A flat-looking body • Poison pincers; hunters • Long legs; many can move fast like a snake	• Two pairs of legs per body segment • Round body segments • No poison pincers; plant eaters • Short legs; creep along slowly

CENTIPEDES / WERI

[Phylum: Arthropoda. Superclass: Myriapoda. Class: Chilopoda]

Centipede means 'one hundred legs', but they usually have 30-354 legs, and never 100 exactly. Because they have more than 6 legs, centipedes are not insects. They avoid light and are active at night. Centipedes are thought to have lived on land for about 400 million years. About 30 species known in New Zealand; about 2,500 known worldwide.

Life cycle: eggs hatch as little centipedes

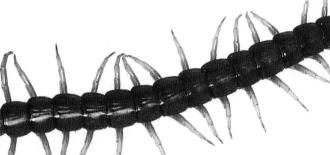

Giant Centipede
Cormocephalus rubriceps

Native New Zealand's largest centipede – up to 25 cm long. Its **bite** can be more painful than a wasp sting. Hunts insects, spiders, worms and even small lizards. Eaten by rats. Found under stones and logs in the North Island and on some offshore islands. Also climbs trees. They live for about 5 years.

House Centipede
Scutigera smithii

Possibly native. Has 30 legs. So that it doesn't 'stand on its own toes', the legs are different lengths. Prefers to live outdoors, but sometimes found in Auckland houses, hunting flies and cockroaches.

Garden Centipede
Lithobius forficatus

Introduced. Found in garden soil. Adult has 30 legs but only 14 when it first hatches from the egg.

MILLIPEDES / WERIMANO

[Phylum: Arthropoda. Superclass: Myriapoda. Class: Diplopoda]

Millipede means 'one thousand legs', but no one has ever found one with more than 752. Because they have more than 6 legs, millipedes are not insects. They have no eyes but avoid light. Feed on fungus and very fine roots. Millipedes are thought to have lived on land for about 400 million years. About 10,000 species known worldwide; about 100 known in New Zealand (of about 600 believed to live here). Most of them are native and are not seen in gardens.

Life cycle: eggs hatch as little millipedes

A Common Native Millipede
Spirobolellus antipodarus [Order: Spirobolida. Family: Spirobolellidae]

Native Picking up one of these can leave a yellow or red stain on your fingers. This is caused by a chemical that many millipedes produce which is poisonous to small animals and distasteful to birds (and to people!) New Zealand robins have even been seen picking up millipedes and brushing them on their feathers as an insecticide.

A Pill Millipede
[Order: Oniscomorpha. Family: Sphaerotheriidae]

Native Curls into a pill-like ball to protect itself from birds and other animals. Found under logs and stones; feeds at night on leaf litter on the forest floor. 5 kinds known in New Zealand.

SLATERS / PĀPAPA

[Phylum: Arthropoda. Superclass: Crustacea. Class: Malacostraca. Order: Isopoda]

Flat creatures with 12 or 14 legs. Because they have more than 6 legs, slaters are not insects. Because of the flat shape and habits of slaters, Māori traditionally grouped these with beetles, giving them the same name. Have been around for over 350 million years. About 50 land species in New Zealand, most of them native; over 4,000 species worldwide. The largest ones alive today live in the sea and grow to 35 cm. Related to shrimps, crabs and crayfish.

Life cycle: eggs hatch as little slaters

Garden Slater
Porcellio scaber

Arrived from Europe before 1847. Known there as woodlice. By day, they hide under leaf litter and stones to stay damp and avoid sunlight. Eat rotting plants, dead animals, sometimes living plants. Eaten by slater spiders (see page 24) and hedgehogs. (Another common garden slater can roll itself into a ball: *Armadillidium vulgare*.)

A Beach Slater
Ligia novaezealandiae [Family: Ligiidae]

Native This slater species is common along soft rocky coasts and clay banks just above the tide. Similar beach slater species are also seen running over sandy beaches.

A Forest Slater
[Family: Oniscidae]

Native Common in leaf litter and under loose bark in native forest.

HOPPERS

[Phylum: Arthropoda. Superclass: Crustacea. Class: Malacostraca. Order: Amphipoda]

Jumping creatures with bodies flattened sideways and 14 legs. Because they have more than 6 legs, hoppers are not insects. Over 100 land-living species thought to live in New Zealand (but few have been named), most living on the ground, though some will climb trees. Over 8,000 worldwide, some living very deep beneath the sea, some in lakes, rivers, along the coastline and in caves. Related to shrimps, crabs and crayfish.

Life cycle: eggs hatch as little hoppers

A Landhopper
Parorchestia tenuis

Native Look like giant fleas. Common on the ground, hopping among damp rotting leaves in native forest, also in farmland and gardens. Eat dead leaves at night. Over 25 named species in New Zealand, all but one of them native.

A Sandhopper
Mōwhiti, Potipoti
Talorchestia quoyana

Native Common on sandy beaches. Help to keep the beach clean by feeding at night on rotting fish and seaweed. Jump about like a large flea, covering over a metre in one leap. Burrow into damp sand. Find their way by checking the angle of the sun. Can give a little nip, but otherwise harmless. About 12 species of sandhoppers known in New Zealand.

LIKE HOPPERS, BUT NOT HOPPERS

Springtails See page 21.

All photos are life-size

VELVET WORMS

Not insects but 'walking worms' with 28-80 legs. A velvet worm (peripatus) hunts by squirting sticky slime from a pair of large glands either side of its mouth. Fossils of similar creatures have been found from 550 million years ago. Thought to be an evolutionary link between worms and centipedes. Well-developed brains. Need moisture. Can be grey, bright green, brown, blue, or purple with orange spots. Over 25 species so far found in New Zealand, all of them native; about 150 known worldwide.
Life cycle: most are born as little velvet worms, but some kinds develop only from eggs

**A Peripatus
Ngāokeoke**
Peripatoides species

Native Found inside rotting logs and under leaf litter in native forest in North and South Islands. Eats worms, insects and spiders. Active at night. Has 15 pairs of legs.

Seem to have '10 Legs or More', but are really Insects

[Phylum: Arthropoda. Class: Insecta]

CATERPILLARS OF BUTTERFLIES & MOTHS

[Order: Lepidoptera]

Caterpillars appear to have 10 legs or more, so how can they still be insects? This is because only the front 6 legs are 'true legs' (jointed with claws and used for gripping food), the 4-10 legs behind these are stubby 'false legs'. Caterpillars all go through a rather magical change (called metamorphosis) to become butterflies or moths. For pictures of the adult butterflies and moths, see pages 4-7.
Life cycle: egg > larva (the caterpillar) > pupa (the chrysalis) > adult butterfly or moth

CATERPILLARS of BUTTERFLIES

Cabbage White Caterpillar
Pieris rapae

Eats leaves of cabbages and other plants of the cabbage family. Also nasturtiums.

Monarch Caterpillar
Danaus plexippus

Eats swan plant leaves.

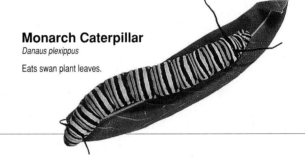

CATERPILLARS of MOTHS

Convolvulus Hawk Caterpillar /Anuhe
Agrius convolvuli

Native Eats leaves of kūmara and other kinds of convolvulus, so has been given many Māori names.

**Greasy Cutworm
Ngūharu, Mūwharu**
Agrotis ipsilon

Native Destroys crops at night, cutting through stems of garden plants, such as kūmara.

**Magpie Moth Caterpillar
Tuahuru**
Nyctemera species

Eats plants in the daisy family, like cineraria and ragwort. Also called 'woolly bear'.

Grapevine Moth Caterpillar
Phalaenoides glycinae

Eats leaves and fruit of grapevines.

Gum Emperor Caterpillar
Opodiphthera eucalypti (formerly *Antheraea eucalypti*)

Eats leaves from gum trees (*Eucalyptus*) and introduced pepper trees (*Schinus*).

Porina Moth Caterpillar
Wiseana species

Native Comes out of the soil at night to eat grass.

**Vegetable Caterpillar
Āwhato, Āwheto**

Native When attacked by a *Cordyceps* fungus, the large ghost moth caterpillar (*Aoraia* species) dies and turns as hard as wood to become a 'vegetable caterpillar'. The caterpillar-shaped part remains underground; only the spore-bearing stalk is seen, poking out of the ground.

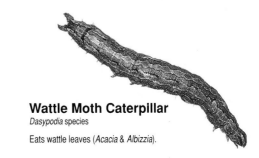

Wattle Moth Caterpillar
Dasypodia species

Eats wattle leaves (*Acacia* & *Albizzia*).

Slimy & Legless

[Phyla: Mollusca, Annelida, Aschelminthes & Platyhelminthes]

SNAILS / NGATA

[Phylum: Mollusca. Class: Gastropod]

Have eyes on the end of long stalks, a tongue covered with sharp teeth, and a coiled shell for protection. Active at night. Most snails are both male and female. They lay eggs from their necks. Can't see but can tell light from dark. With about 1,200 species (most of them native), New Zealand has more land snails for its size than most other countries in the world. Some can be as much as 10 cm across, but most are tiny (1-5 mm across).

Life cycle: eggs hatch as little snails

Superb Land Snail
Powelliphanta superba

Native New Zealand's largest land snail – can be 10 cm across. Lives in deep leaf mould in cool, wet native forest near Nelson. Eats mostly earthworms, also slugs. Eaten by weka, rats, possums and wild pigs. Usually active at night. Can live 40 years.

Hochstetter's Land Snail
Powelliphanta hochstetteri

Native Found only in high forest near Nelson. Eats mostly earthworms (left).

Kauri Snail
Pūpū Rangi
Paryphanta busbyi

Native Can be 8 cm across. Climbs trees. Used to be common up in kauri trees, but now found mostly on the ground in damp scrub and fern. Found north of Auckland. Can travel several hundred metres in one night. Eats mostly earthworms. Eaten by possums and wild pigs.

Flax Snail
Pūpū Harakeke
Placostylus species

Native On wet nights, eats freshly fallen leaves. (Karaka leaves are a favourite.) Found near the coast in leaf litter only at northern tip of the North Island and on some northern offshore islands. Young snails climb trees and hide under the leaves. Territorial. Eaten by pigs and rats. Some shells are white (albino).

Hochstetter's land snail eating a native earthworm

World's Largest Land Snail

The body of one West African giant snail, *Achatina achatina*, measured 39.3 cm and weighed exactly 900 g. Its shell was 27.3 cm across.

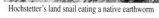 

Small Native Land Snails

Native Live in damp places in native forest, among leaf litter, under flaking bark and rotting wood. Easy to find on rotting nīkau leaves. Many climb high into trees and hide on the underside of leaves. Eat mostly mould and algae. About 1,200 species known, their shells of many different colours, patterns and shapes, most just 1-5 mm across.

Brown Garden Snail
Cornu aspersum (formerly *Helix aspersa*)

One of 7 or 8 species of introduced snail found in New Zealand gardens or around pot plants. Others are much smaller. Eats plants. Can climb trees. Sometimes heard at night scraping their 15,000 teeth on mould-covered windows. Top speed: 10 cm/min. Fire tiny 'love darts' at each other when they want to mate. Some French people eat them.

All photos are life-size

SLUGS / PUTOKO
[Phylum: Mollusca. Class: Gastropoda]

...ugs are like snails without the outside shell. Live only in damp places. The slime stops them drying out. All slugs are both male and female. Like snails, they lay eggs ...m their necks, have eyes on the end of long stalks which can't see but which can tell light from dark. Also have a tongue covered with sharp teeth. Active at night. Most ...t plants and fungi. About a dozen kinds found in New Zealand gardens (most from Europe); over 25 species of native slugs found in or near native forest or scrub.
...e cycle: eggs hatch as little slugs

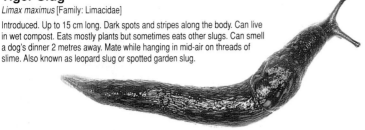

Tiger Slug
Limax maximus [Family: Limacidae]

Introduced. Up to 15 cm long. Dark spots and stripes along the body. Can live in wet compost. Eats mostly plants but sometimes eats other slugs. Can smell a dog's dinner 2 metres away. Mate while hanging in mid-air on threads of slime. Also known as leopard slug or spotted garden slug.

Grey Field Slug
Deroceras reticulatum [Family: Limacidae]

Introduced. Almost white underneath. Common. Has a good sense of smell. Lives on or near the soil surface and doesn't burrow. Can travel at 10 metres an hour.

breathing hole

A Leafveined Slug
[Family: Athoracophoridae]

Native About 25 kinds known, all flat with a pattern on the back like veins of a leaf. Breathe through a hole in the top of their body. Most climb high into the trees in dark, damp native forest, scraping off any fungi and algae they find growing on leaves. Eaten by rats. Some kinds can be 15 cm long, but most are smaller.

Orangesoled Slug
Arion hortensis [Family: Arionidae]

Introduced, but found in damaged native forest as well as in gardens. Foot has yellow or orange sole. Can burrow 30 cm underground.

EARTHWORMS / TOKE, NOKE
[Phylum: Annelida. Class: Oligochaeta]

...ve mostly underground, eating soil and pieces of plants. Can sense light but have no eyes. Each worm is both male and female. Find each other by ...ell. Have 5 pairs of hearts. When cut, can often regrow a new tail. Have been around for over 500 million years. More than 3,200 species worldwide; ...er 200 in New Zealand, about 20 of these being introduced worms found in gardens and farmland. The 180 or so native earthworms include dark-...loured ones found on the surface among leaf litter and the long, pale-coloured 'milkworms' which live much deeper down.
...fe cycle: eggs hatch as little worms. (Only the adult has the 'saddle'.)

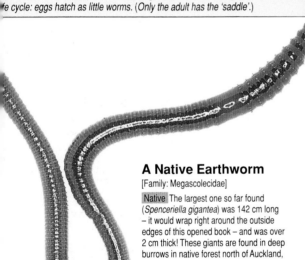

A Native Earthworm
[Family: Megascolecidae]

Native The largest one so far found (*Spenceriella gigantea*) was 142 cm long – it would wrap right around the outside edges of this opened book – and was over 2 cm thick! These giants are found in deep burrows in native forest north of Auckland, and on several offshore islands such as Little Barrier, Great Barrier and Kawau Islands. The worm illustrated is a smaller, more common, native species. Eaten by early Māori.

Common Earthworm
Allolobophora caliginosa [Family: Lumbricidae]

Introduced. Common in gardens and fields in autumn and winter. Live in the top 15 cm of soil.

Tiger Earthworm
Eisenia fetida [Family: Lumbricidae]

Introduced. Found in wet compost. Need sour conditions and can't survive in normal soil. Sometimes sold for compost-making.

GORDIAN WORMS / ENGAIO
[Phylum: Aschelminthes. Class: Nematomorpha]

...ound in ditches, ponds and streams. Looks like wriggling spaghetti, tying itself in knots. ...ays eggs in water. Larvae hatch, are eaten by water insects and live as a parasite inside the ...sect's body until big enough to enter the water again. Adult worm never eats. The odd one ...nds its way through the water supply and out the kitchen tap. Nobody knows how many ...ecies there are in New Zealand; over 250 worldwide.
...fe cycle: egg > larva > adult gordian worm

A Gordian Worm

FLATWORMS
[Phylum: Platyhelminthes]

Like a flattened slug. Live in damp soil, leaf litter and rotting wood, eating earthworms, snails and other small soil animals. Each flatworm is both male and female. About 200 species of land flatworms in New Zealand, some bright yellow, others blue, red, brown or green; over 3,000 worldwide.
Life cycle: eggs hatch as little flatworms

A Common Flatworm
Caenoplana coerulea

Introduced from Australia. Common in the North Island.

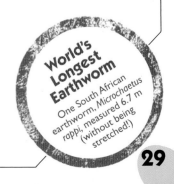

World's Longest Earthworm
One South African earthworm, *Microchaetus rappi*, measured 6.7 m (without being stretched!)

What Did That?

INSECT & SPIDER EGGS

Eggs of a
Ladybird
Illeis galbula

See page 8.

Egg case of a
New Zealand Praying Mantis
Orthodera novaezealandiae

See page 20.

Egg case of a
South African Praying Mantis
Miomantis caffra

See page 20.

Damage to twig
from eggs laid by a
Cicada
Amphipsalta species

See page 19.

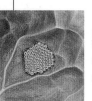

Eggs of a **Green Vegetable Bug**
Nezara viridula

See page 19.

Eggs of a
Giant Wētā
Deinacrida heteracantha

See page 10.

Egg case of a
Cottony Cushion Scale Insect
Icerya purchasi

See page 19.

Egg sac of a
Garden Orbweb Spider
Eriophora pustulosa

See page 22.

Egg case of a
Cockroach
Periplaneta species

See page 20.

Damage to twig
from eggs laid by a
Passionvine Hopper
Scolypopa australis

See page 19.

INSECT NESTS

Nest of an
Australian Paper Wasp
Polistes humilis

See page 17.

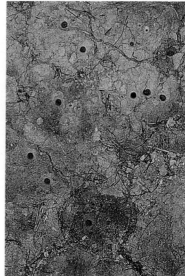

Hole in the ground made by
A Hunting Wasp
[Family: Sphecidae]

See page 17.

Holes in the ground made by nesting
Tiger Beetles
Neocicindela tuberculata

See page 9.

Nest of a
Chinese Paper Wasp
Polistes chinensis

See page 17.

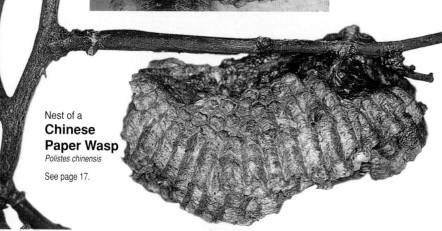

Nest of a
Mason Wasp
Pison spinolae

See page 17.

Hole in the ground
made by
A Native Bee
[Family: Colletidae]

See page 16.

30

All photos are life-size

Cocoon of a
Gum Emperor Moth
Opodiphthera eucalypti
See page 6.

Pupa of a
**Greasy
Cutworm**
Agrotis ipsilon
See page 7.

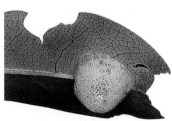

Empty nymph
case of a
Cicada
[Family: Cicadidae]
See page 19.

Pupa (chrysalis)
of a
**Monarch
Butterfly**
Danaus plexippus
See page 5.

Bag of a
**Common
Bag Moth**
Liothula omnivora
See page 7.

Cuckoo spit made by
the nymphs of the
Spittle Bug
[Family: Cercopidae]
See page 19.

INSECTS OR MITES EATING

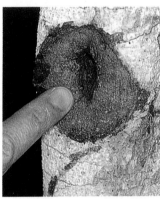

Hole in tree trunk
made by the
caterpillar of a
Pūriri Moth
Aenetus virescens
See page 6.

Paper eaten by a
Silverfish
Lepisma saccharina
See page 21.

Holes in kawakawa leaf
made by caterpillar of a
**Kawakawa
Looper Moth**
Cleora scriptaria [Family: Geometridae]

Damage by
the common
House Borer
Anobium punctatum
(a tiny beetle)

Leaf damage made by the
Pōhutukawa Psyllid
Trioza curta [Family: Triozidae]

Stem gall on
lacebark branch made by the
Lacebark Gall Mite
Eriophyes hoheriae

Rust fungus gall on wattle,
eaten by
A Fungus Weevil
Araecerus palmaris

and the caterpillar of a
Wattle Gall Moth
Gauna aegusalis [Family: Pyralidae]

Stem gall in catsear plant
made by the tiny
Catsear Gall Wasp
Phanacis hypochoeridis

Index

Where there are several page numbers, the bold numbers show the main entry.